THE WORLD JESUS KNEW

MOODY PRESS
CHICAGO

ISBN 0-8024-2480-5

Book design and layout: Peter Wyart
Three's Company

Worldwide coedition organized and
produced by
Angus Hudson Ltd,
Concorde House, Grenville Place,
Mill Hill, London NW7 3SA, England
Tel +44 208 9459 3668
Fax +44 208 9459 3678
email: coed@angushudson.com

PICTURE ACKNOWLEDGMENTS

Photographs
Tim Dowley: pp. 17, 25, 29, 37, 49, 59, 64,
65, 66, 69, 71, 76, 82A, 90, 91, 93, 137, 141,
146, 173, 175, 183
Peter Wyart: pp. 18, 36, 38, 50, 57, 70, 72,
75, 77, 78, 79, 80, 82, 84, 89, 95, 121, 179
Israel Government Press Office
  Maggi Ayalon: p. 157
  Anker Einmat: p. 115 right
  Amos ben Gershom: pp. 34, 37, 83
  Arik Hermoni: p. 7
  Ziv Koren: pp. 99, 113
  Moshe Milner: pp. 85, 101, 114, 125, 140,
    145, 151
  Avi Ohayon: pp. 1, 3, 47, 115 left, 126, 131,
    135, 149, 155
  Ya'acov Sa'ar: pp. 21, 23, 111

Illustrations
Jeremy Gower: pp. 24, 44
James Macdonald: pp. 13, 151
Richard Scott: pp. 35, 39, 41, 107

Moody Press, a ministry of the Moody Bible
Institute, is designed for education,
evangelization, and edification. If we may
assist you in knowing more about Christ and
the Christian life, please write us without
obligation:
Moody Press
c/o MLM
Chicago, Illinois 60610, USA

THE WORLD
JESUS KNEW

ANNE PUNTON

MOODY PRESS
CHICAGO

ACKNOWLEDGEMENTS

Many experiences and people have made this book possible but some must have specific acknowledgement.

First is Walter Riggans. He made time in a very busy schedule to read the various drafts of the book carefully and offer comments and suggestions. Because his expertise in theological and related matters is far greater than mine, I have immensely valued his appraisal. In almost every case I adopted his suggestions but in the few instances where I did not, he graciously let me have the last word. Above all, at every stage he offered unbounded encouragement. I value both his friendship and help and thank him deeply for everything. Any errors or shortcomings are the author's alone.

In 1992 I took early retirement and joined my mother in her bungalow in Snaith, North Humberside. Shortly before I arrived, she had a small extension added to make a study for me. She died a year later but I never enter this quiet room, looking out on to the secluded back garden, without thinking of her. I praise God for her loving foresight.

Nor do I ever start a writing session without thanking God that the multiple sclerosis, which forced me into early retirement, has not slowed down my mental abilities or affected my eyes and that I can still type easily. I do not take God's goodness for granted.

I have left Jack to the last. He is my husband and we first met when I came to Snaith. Much to our own and everyone else's surprise, we found ourselves engaged to be married shortly after my mother's death. He had no difficulty in keeping the kitchen functioning, coffee flowing and the dog in order, while I virtually ignored him to concentrate on writing. Well, as a confirmed widower for sixteen years and with six children and numerous grandchildren, he is well experienced in coping with situations and people. He is a wonderful man and I love him and owe him more than I can say for all his unobtrusive, strong support.

Anne Punton
September 1996

CONTENTS

INTRODUCTION

The Bible speaks to us all in the west today but it is not a product of today's western society. It is basically a Middle Eastern book which was written many centuries ago. It reflects the cultures and world views of peoples whose ways were quite different from ours. Above all, it mirrors the world of the Israelites and of the Jewish people from the Babylonian exile to the time of the apostles.

To understand the Bible more fully, we must read it with an awareness of all its original contexts. Obviously, the more we know about the ways of those times and places, and in particular of the Jewish world, the greater our appreciation of its stories, characters and teaching will be.

For instance, we only grasp the full impact of many passages when we discern some of the nuances of the Greek and Hebrew languages in which they are written. Hebrew thought, culture and religious values underlie the way in which even the Greek language is used in the New Testament. After all, apart from Luke, the writers were Jews. Although Luke was probably not Jewish by birth, the evidence suggests that he was a Jewish proselyte or, at least, someone who was deeply influenced by Jewish spirituality and the Jewish Bible.

Some scholars note how often Hebrew and Aramaic idioms occur in the style of Greek used by New Testament writers. They feel that certain books, such as Mark's gospel, were perhaps first written in Hebrew and only later translated into Greek. The importance of Hebrew, and Greek too, cannot be over-emphasised. Without doubt, translations of the Bible are a great gift from God but something is always lost in a translation.

Our comprehension of certain passages and events is also enhanced when we know their historical background. Social, agricultural, religious and other customs condition events and the behaviour of people in specific situations. Even climate and geography, so different from that in the western world, play a part in determining what happens and why.

Many of Jesus' parables which are based on agricultural images only make sense when we understand the oriental ways of working the land or caring for livestock. These ways are rarely the same as those of western farmers, more especially in modern times when everything is so mechanised.

Rabbinic traditions preserve a record of how Judaism functioned during the Second Temple period, both preceding and during the life of Jesus. The New Testament takes it for granted that its readers know all about these things, but we, today, do not.

When we learn, for example, about the magnificent pageantry of the Temple festivities, it opens up a rich, new dimension to the ministry of Jesus, as we shall later see. A case in point is the Feast of Tabernacles. A rich symbolism, associated with water and light, underlies the elaborate rituals of that festival. As we learn about this, suddenly the full power of Jesus' words, recorded in John 7 and 8, dawns upon us.

The Bible did not come to us in a vacuum, nor was God's choice of the Jewish people a mere whim. Salvation does not depend on a good knowledge of the background of its contents, but any moving forward to a mature grasp of the Scriptures cannot take place without such knowledge. In general, then, this book seeks to inform modern, western readers about such issues. In particular, we are concerned to deepen our appreciation of Jesus himself.

The chapters each cover a distinct aspect of the life of Jesus as we examine his birth, childhood and education, the way he dressed, the languages he spoke, prayers he would have said, and much more. The method used is to portray specific aspects of his life and then,

An Eastern shepherd rests beneath the shade of an old fig tree. The Bible is basically a Middle Eastern book and reflects the world views of peoples different from ourselves.

from this base, to branch out into numerous highways and byways, taking time to traverse many different areas of the whole Bible record. Along the way we shall see how the Christian faith springs uniquely from solid, biblical, Jewish roots.

There are one or two occasions when we refer to a place called Palestine. In the light of events in the Middle East during the latter part of the twentieth century, this name has become a politically loaded term. We must emphasise that on no occasion does any use of the word Palestine imply a political bias.

The Romans first used the appellation, Palestine, to describe the territory along the eastern Mediterranean seaboard. The southern part of that coast had long been inhabited by the Philistines and their descendants, from whom the name is derived. In the historical and geographical context of this book, the usage is correct. However, in consideration of any sensitivity amongst our readers, we avoid frequent use of the word and substitute some other descriptive phrase.

We are also careful in our use of the word Bible. For Christians, the Bible contains the Hebrew Old Testament and the Greek New Testament. The Jewish Bible consists only of the former. Moreover, the title Old Testament is offensive to Jewish people in its implications. The chapter on the Scriptures explains this more fully. At present, we simply point out that we try to make the necessary distinctions by talking about the Hebrew Bible or the Jewish Scriptures in references to the Old Testament.

Throughout the book we use the abbreviations BCE (Before the Common Era) for the times before Jesus and CE (Common Era) for the years after his coming. This is done in accordance with a growing scholarly consensus which prefers this neutral terminology to the directly Christian convention of using BC and AD. It enables Jewish and Christian people to work more easily together. In part, it marks the fact that some of the best research being done today into the original contexts of the life of Jesus is by Jewish scholars. We certainly do not underestimate the significance of the coming of Jesus into the world or lack confidence in the power of the Gospel.

We give biblical references where appropriate but do not provide references to rabbinic sources or to the writings of people like Josephus because we do not anticipate that many of our readers will have access to such works. If they do, they will doubtless already have some knowledge of matters covered in this book and will be able to use the appropriate indices to trace any further information required.

Scripture references come from the Jerusalem Bible unless stated otherwise. Quotations from Jewish prayers are taken from the Hertz edition of the Authorised Jewish Daily Prayer Book, bearing in mind that for many of these prayers, the traditional English usage is almost as fixed as the original Hebrew and varies very little from one edition of the Prayer Book to the next.

CHAPTER ONE

A Word About Sources

Before ever we can embark on a work like this, we must answer one vital question. Where do we find the information which makes such a book possible?

Material comes from many sources and we cannot use all that is available. Nor can the accuracy of everything be guaranteed. For example, archaeological discoveries must be interpreted, the historian Josephus is known to exaggerate, rabbinic records sometimes offer the slightly divergent recollections of two different sages. No matter! The overall picture which emerges is as authentic as it is possible to be.

Historical Records

Bible history is part of Middle Eastern history. It is revealed in diverse forms; the writings of ancient historians, the deciphering of clay tablets, hieroglyphic carvings and pictures on the remains of buildings unearthed by archaeologists, papyrus documents and even the traditions and legends of local peoples. Archaeological digs disclose houses, temples, synagogues, city streets, public baths, sports stadia, sewage and irrigation systems, pottery, jewellery, artefacts, mosaics, tombs and much more. All these things help to make up the jig-

saw picture of everyday life in the ancient world.

We are indebted to many writers for information but the two to whom we most often

The Rosetta Stone, the discovery of which gave a key to Egyptian hieroglyphics.

refer are Philo and Josephus. Philo of Alexandria (*c*.20 BCE–50 CE) was a Jewish philosopher rather than a historian but his works contain many passages which shed light on biblical matters. Flavius Josephus (*c*.37–100 CE) was a prolific Jewish author who wrote about every Jewish topic imaginable. His documentation of the historical events through which he lived in first century Palestine (as the country was then called) is invaluable to both secular historians and Bible scholars alike.

If archaeological finds from the ancient worlds of Chaldea, Assyria, Babylonia, Egypt and other vanished empires shed light on Bible days, so too do the writings of the old historians. Those listed below are not quoted in this book but much of what is known about the Bible world comes from these and similar sources.

For instance, the Greek Herodotus (born *c*.490 BCE) chronicled the conflict between Greece and Persia. He travelled widely, especially in Egypt, and incorporated all the information he could find about the known world of that time into his works. Into that context comes the close of the Jewish Exile in Babylonia and events immediately following.

The Roman Tacitus (*c*.55–117 CE) wrote a two part history of the Roman Empire and its early emperors. This is the background against which we view the New Testament record. The Roman historian Seutonius (*c*.69–mid 2nd century CE) refers to people who are mentioned in the New Testament. As a result we can date happenings very accurately, especially those connected with Paul.

Eusebius (*c*.260–340 CE) was a native and bishop of Caesarea. Despite his later dates, his value as an early church historian lies in the fact that he carefully studied and drew upon earlier sources which were close to the times in question.

Language, Geography, Culture and Tradition

Apart from a few portions in Aramaic, the original languages of the Bible are Hebrew in the Old Testament and Greek in the New Testament. Any translation always loses some of the finer meaning of the original and the Bible is no exception. Jewish rabbis are quick to discover new biblical insights through their knowledge of Hebrew. The careful distinctions of the numerous Greek prepositions and tenses can also add illuminating nuances to many a passage. Even for those who are not linguistic experts, some parts of this book might help to open up the Scriptures through this way.

The geography of an area is important too. If we know about the climate of Bible lands, we know what time of year certain events took place. For example, when Jesus saw the fields ripe for harvest it was spring and not autumn, as western readers might deduce.

Topography determines the strategic importance of some places for military security or trade. King Solomon built a fortress at Megiddo, which overlooks a pass through the hills from the coast to the Jezreel plain inland.[1] From ancient days to General Allenby in the early twentieth century, the world's armies have used this route. Here, we are told, will be the site of the last great conflict, Armageddon or the battle of Har (mount) Megiddo.[2]

The reason why Ahab constantly fought over Ramoth Gilead was because it was direct-

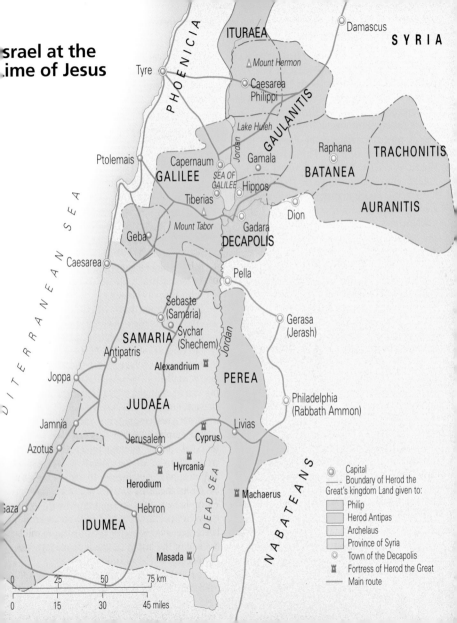

Israel at the Time of Jesus

PHOENICIA
ITURAEA
△ Mount Hermon
Damascus
SYRIA

Tyre
Caesarea Philippi
GAULANITIS

Lake Huleh
Jordan
Ptolemais
Capernaum
Gamala
Raphana
TRACHONITIS

GALILEE
SEA OF GALILEE
BATANEA

Hippos
AURANITIS

Tiberias
Dion

Mount Tabor
Gadara
DECAPOLIS

Geba

Caesarea

Pella

Sebaste (Samaria)
Gerasa (Jerash)

Sychar (Shechem)
SAMARIA

Antipatris
Jordan

Alexandrium ⌂
PEREA

Joppa

JUDAEA
Philadelphia (Rabbath Ammon)

Jamnia
Livias

Azotus
Jerusalem
Cyprus ⌂

Hycania ⌂
Hyrcania ⌂

Herodium ⌂
⌂ Machaerus

Gaza
Hebron

IDUMEA
DEAD SEA

Masada ⌂

NABATEANS

◎ Capital
Boundary of Herod the Great's kingdom Land given to:
Philip
Herod Antipas
Archelaus
Province of Syria
◎ Town of the Decapolis
⌂ Fortress of Herod the Great
Main route

0	25	50	75 km

0	15	30	45 miles

ly on the Kings' Highway, the main trade route along the plateau east of the river Jordan.[3] To the north it led to Damascus and thence to Asia Minor or to countries in the fertile crescent formed by the Euphrates and Tigris rivers. Southwards it joined routes into Egypt, Africa, Arabia and the Far East. Roads branched off across Palestine to the Mediterranean. Whoever owned Ramoth Gilead controlled trade in every direction.

Cultural, social and everyday routines have barely changed in the Middle East from ancient times. Only in our own century are western technology and lifestyles slowly replacing the old customs. Even today, especially in poorer, secluded areas, traditional ways of doing things still persist. So, when the Bible talks of a threshing sledge with teeth, a burden bearer or a water seller, we know exactly what is meant because we can still see these things today.

'Tradition' is a key word in the life of the Middle East. Things have been done in the same way for countless ages. People have used the same tools, worn the same clothes and perpetuated the same habits from one generation to another. Only in the twentieth century have the old ways been eroded by the introduction of western technology, standards and lifestyle. Notwithstanding, there are still isolated villages, invariably Arab, where western influence has barely penetrated and where the tourists do not go. There, the general way of life and such things as agricultural equipment and methods remain the same as in Bible times.

Fortunately, a few Bible-loving travellers who visited the Holy Land last century recognised what they were seeing and recorded their findings in words, paintings and collections of artefacts. Little did they know how soon the traditions of time immemorial would be modified or swept away by twentieth century innovation. How important their records now are for an understanding of everyday life in Bible times.

Traditions of the Elders

There is, however, a further source of biblical understanding. Judaism has preserved a large body of ancient traditions about how religious life was regulated in the Second Temple period (c.520 BCE–70 CE). As even secular life was subjected to religious law, these traditions reveal a great deal about the everyday affairs of ordinary people.

This is of great value when we try to imagine the private, daily life of Jesus. The gospel narratives take knowledge of these things for granted and see no reason to explain them. We do not necessarily need this extra information, but Scripture is immeasurably enriched when we can fill in some of the details behind what is happening.

The rabbinic records are particularly rich in matters to do with the Temple, the festivals and ritual purity. All these topics are referred to in the Gospels. We can look back to Leviticus and Numbers for some elucidation but it is the rabbis who tell us the details of how things worked in practice. So important are the 'traditions of the elders', as the Gospels call them, for a fuller comprehension of the times of Jesus, that we ought to know briefly how they developed.

A nineteenth century illustration of veiled Jews reading from the Torah.

From Torah to Mishnah

The source of Jewish belief and practice is the Law or Torah. It was given by God at Sinai and is recorded in the first five books of the Bible. It was soon apparent that some matters needed elucidation. For example, the Torah allowed a bill of divorce; but what form should it take and how should it be administered? The Law ordained rejoicing at the Feast of Tabernacles with palms, willows, fruit of goodly trees and leafy branches; but exactly what fruit and leafy branches were meant and how should one rejoice with them?

In answering such questions, a body of explanatory, oral tradition accumulated around the written Law. Before long, the Oral Torah, as it was called, became as binding as the Written Torah.

Israel exchanged its nomadic existence for a settled, agricultural way of life under a king and with a Temple. Then followed the exile and subsequent return to the land, but no longer as an independent, sovereign nation. The second Temple was erected and the synagogue became an established institution.

Throughout these changes, the Oral Torah grew apace, keeping step with the history of the nation. Men of phenomenal memory devoted their lives to studying, memorising and teaching it. They were called the Tanna'im and many of the religious leaders of Jesus' day were of their number.

Only after the destruction of the second Temple (70 CE) and a failed revolt against Rome (131–135 CE) did two serious problems threaten the Oral Law. Firstly, it had become such an unwieldy body of material that it challenged even the most accurate memory. Secondly, the Jewish people were so decimated that many of the scholars had either died or were scattered throughout the diaspora. There was a real danger that much of it would be lost.

A rabbi called Judah the Prince therefore decided to write it down. He and his followers made it their lives' work to classify and record all the important oral traditions which stood alongside the Written Torah. By 200 CE their work, called the Mishnah, was complete. The Mishnah is divided into six parts. Its contents are complicated and often abstruse. An English version comprises one thick, closely written book of heavy, legalistic material.

Although the Oral Torah was a kind of commentary on the Written Torah, the Mishnah deals with subjects which appear mainly in the book of Leviticus. It covers things like sacrifice, priesthood, leprosy, food laws, ritual purity, festivals, Temple practice, agriculture, tithes, offerings, marriage, divorce, adultery, civil rights, vows and more. It tells us what the traditions of the elders were all about and how religious affairs were conducted in Second Temple times. The Mishnah, therefore, reveals and explains much of the religious context in which Jesus and his compatriots lived.

Although we must emphasise that the rabbinic traditions were written down much later than both the times to which they refer and the New Testament documents themselves, this does not invalidate their usefulness. Many societies have recorded their own, ancient, oral traditions and it is generally accepted that such material is handed down through many generations, by word of mouth, with considerable accuracy.

The rabbinic traditions preserve a record of how Judaism functioned during the Second Temple period. Naturally, we must use some caution and discernment but, overall, we can be reasonably sure that the contents of the Mishnah reliably reflect the way of life in New Testament times. This is particularly so where certain customs, facts or events are corroborated from other sources.

Rabbinic Insights

Over the years, the rabbis have studied this foundation text of Judaism to produce the Talmud and many other classical works. Their method of study is combative. Two or more people open up a passage in a face-to-face confrontation with question, answer, counter question, argument, logic and even an element of one upmanship. The exercise sharpens the mind. It means that when the rabbis look at the Jewish Scriptures, they see them differently from most Christians.

In this connection, we must note that the New Testament is not part of the Jewish Bible. Jewish scholars and rabbis have not traditionally given their attention to the Christian Scriptures. Only in recent times are a few beginning to do so. When they do, their thoughts on familiar passages are well worth considering.

As far as their own Scriptures are concerned, the rabbis offer many interesting and unusual insights. Some, though fascinating,

Development of the Oral Torah

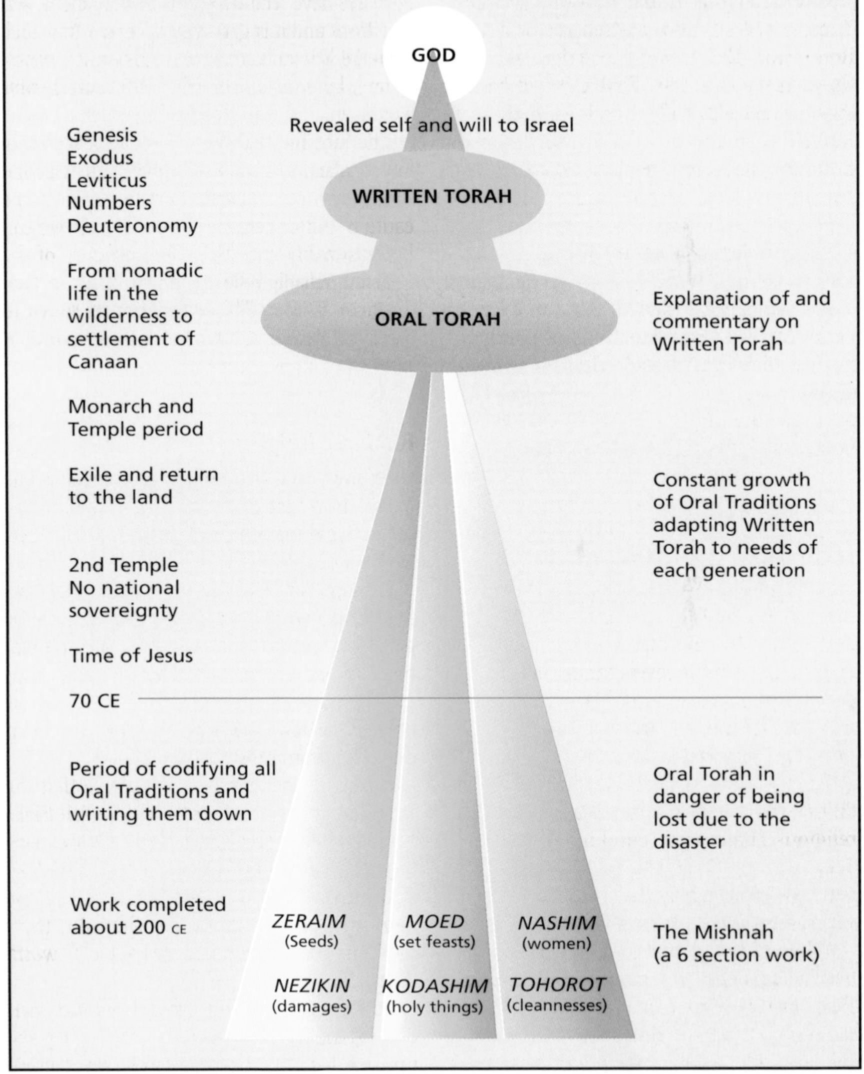

GOD

Revealed self and will to Israel

WRITTEN TORAH

Genesis
Exodus
Leviticus
Numbers
Deuteronomy

ORAL TORAH

From nomadic
life in the
wilderness to
settlement of
Canaan

Explanation of and
commentary on
Written Torah

Monarch and
Temple period

Exile and return
to the land

Constant growth
of Oral Traditions
adapting Written
Torah to needs of
each generation

2nd Temple
No national
sovereignty

Time of Jesus

70 CE

Period of codifying all
Oral Traditions and
writing them down

Oral Torah in
danger of being
lost due to the
disaster

Work completed
about 200 CE

ZERAIM
(Seeds)

MOED
(set feasts)

NASHIM
(women)

The Mishnah
(a 6 section work)

NEZIKIN
(damages)

KODASHIM
(holy things)

TOHOROT
(cleannesses)

are not greatly significant. Have you ever wondered what fruit Adam and Eve really did eat? How about the fig, seeing that they later used fig leaves to cover their nakedness? If we take the story literally, then a fig is as likely as an apple. The climate is too hot in that part of the world for apples to grow well except on high ground.

Many of their understandings have great spiritual value, such as their discussion on the laws of leprosy. When Miriam spoke against Moses behind his back, she contracted leprosy for a week as a punishment.[4] The rabbis therefore associate gossip and criticism with this disease.

In Hebrew, the link between scandal and leprosy is reinforced. A leper is a *metzora*. One who speaks evil is a *motzira*. It is quite permissible, in the rabbinic way of thinking, to take words which sound alike and to establish some homiletical link between them. Setting aside any discussion on a possible connection between sin and illness, we can certainly see the importance of pointing out the dangers of what the rabbis call 'an evil tongue'.

In the chapters which now follow, we shall draw on all the sources mentioned above to present a picture of Jesus in his own times.

Bible references

1 1 Kings 9:15
2 Revelation 16:16
3 1 Kings 22:1–4
4 Numbers 12:1–16

CHAPTER TWO

The Home Jesus Entered

The record of the birth and childhood of Jesus strongly illustrates his Jewishness and the Jewish, biblical milieu in which he was reared. The genealogies, the Zechariah and Elizabeth story, Mary and Joseph's betrothal, the circumcision, the Simeon narrative and the later events in the Temple all make this clear. Despite the brevity of the gospel narrative, we can enlarge the picture from a knowledge of the sources.

The old souk, or market, Nazareth.

Born in Bethlehem

Being so familiar with the stories about Jesus' birth, we rarely think to ask what Mary and Joseph were doing in Nazareth when their family background was originally in Bethlehem. A possible answer to the question lies in the history of the region.

When Alexander the Great died (321 BCE), his vast conquests were divided between his four generals. This left the geographical area along the Mediterranean coastline, which was strategically placed between Egypt and countries in the north, constantly under the control of one or other warring faction. The Seleucid dynasty, which controlled Galilee for a time, attempted to eradicate the Jewish religion. As a result, many Galilean Jews fled to Judaea in search of religious liberty.

Eventually, the Maccabean Jewish freedom fighters overthrew the foreign dictators and established their own ruling dynasty. Under one of their strongest kings, Alexander Yannai (126–76 BCE), some of the Galilean families who had settled in Judaea returned home. They tended to be religious nationalists, perhaps even Zealots, who were anxious to reclaim Galilee for the Jewish people. A few Judaean Jews who actively endorsed their cause also joined the resettlement movement. Was this Mary and Joseph's background? As direct descendants of King David, did their forebears move to Galilee with the messianic hope of one day restoring the whole kingdom to a Davidic dynasty and even to their own kin? It is a credible theory which raises interesting speculations about the family ethos in which Jesus was nurtured.

Genealogies

Tracing ancestry is a very Jewish thing to do. Various genealogical lists appear in the Hebrew Scriptures which greatly aid our understanding of certain events. Even today, one meets Jewish people who proudly trace their family tree over many generations. A genealogy of Jesus' descent from King David was, and still is, an important witness to his messiahship. Perhaps most commentators agree that Matthew[1] gives Joseph's ancestry and Luke[2] gives Mary's.

Joseph goes back to David through the kings of Judah. This is important because, although he was not the biological father of Jesus, he was his legal guardian. Actually, if Joseph had been Jesus' father, his kingly descent would have debarred him from the messianic promises. When Judah went into captivity to Babylon (587 BCE) and the monarchy ended, God disqualified the royal line from any further role in the following way.

King Josiah had three sons and a grandson who all reigned in a complicated series of succession.[3] The monarchy might have contin-

ued through any one of them. From any one of them the Messiah might reasonably have been expected to come.

As it happened, Jehoahaz died in Egypt. Jehoiakim died in prison in Babylon. After a short rule his son, Jehoiachin or Coniah, was also taken captive to Babylon. Although he was eventually pardoned, he never reigned again. Zedekiah saw his sons killed before his eyes before he, too, died in Babylon. It is from Coniah that the royal line continues down to Joseph.[4]

This is where the disqualification clause comes into play. Concerning Coniah God said, 'List this man as "Childless" . . . since none of his descendants will have the fortune to sit on the throne of David or to rule in Judah again'.[5] Neither a political nor a messianic direct descendant of Coniah can ever succeed to David's throne.

Zerubbabel, Coniah's grandson, was a recognised leader who brought the first wave of exiles back to Jerusalem but he never ruled as king.[6] From him the line continued through private individuals but none of them held royal office. King Alexander Yannai and other rulers of the Hasmonean dynasty came from the tribe of Levi. King Herod the Great was an Idumaean (i.e. from Edom) and only a convert to Judaism.

Mary, too, traced her ancestry to David, but not by the kings. She goes back to Nathan who was the son of David and Bathsheba and full brother to Solomon.[7] There is, however, a problem. The genealogies of both Mary and Joseph meet in the persons of Zerubbabel and his father, Shealtiel. In Matthew, Shealtiel is son of Coniah.[8] In Luke he is son of Neri.[9] Because we assume that Zerubbabel and

How Jesus Traces his Ancestry to David

A possible solution to the problem posed by the two different genealogies

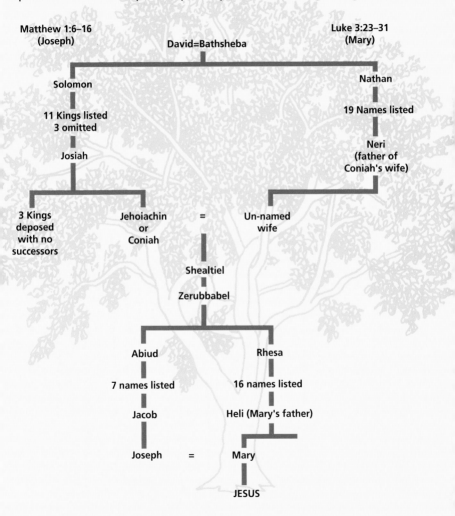

Shealtiel are the same two people in both lists, two questions arise which are not easy to answer adequately.

Firstly, if Mary is descended from Coniah and the kings, through Shealtiel and Zerubbabel, surely her offspring also comes under the ban? What we need to remember is that Mary's line must have come down to her father from one of Zerubbabel's younger sons. Unlike Joseph's, it was not direct. More to the point, Mary was a woman and women rarely counted in such calculations. In both cases her descent from Coniah had no significance as far as the disqualification was concerned.

Secondly, we must then ask, who was Neri? What seems to happen is that Luke's genealogy twice branches out along a female route. It starts with Mary herself and goes back through her father to Zerubbabel and Shealtiel. Then, instead of going to Shealtiel's father, Coniah, it goes to his mother and back through her father to reach Nathan and David. The route is valid but it is inconspicuous.

By virtue of the very obscurity of that line, Jesus is more clearly seen to be the one and only true son of David by the flesh whose kingly, messianic claims are acceptable. Few truths about Jesus are immediately obvious or according to patterns of normal logic. He even taught in parables. Much is concealed and only becomes clear as his followers study to understand. In this sense, his hidden lineage also accords well with the obscurity and mysteries of his birth.

Friends and Relations

The Zechariah story fits into the chapter on the Temple, but we ask one question here. Was there a priestly link in Jesus' ancestry? Mary was related to Elizabeth, wife of Zechariah, a priest.[10] Priests were expected to marry within the clan and Elizabeth definitely came from a priestly family.[11] Was Mary's father descended from David and her mother from Aaron? Whatever way Mary and Elizabeth's relationship is worked out, it suggests a fortuitous insight into the priestly role of Jesus as well as the kingly.

An ancient, Syriac, Christian tradition claims that Mary and Salome, wife of Zebedee, were sisters. We do not know if this is correct but if so, it would make Jesus, James and John to be cousins. At least one scholar suggests that John was a priest.

The disciple who followed the trial of Jesus is generally taken to be John. He knew the high priest well enough to have access to his premises and to bring the unknown Peter in as well.[12] John's gospel focuses on incidents in the Temple. Scenes in his book of the Revelation are reminiscent of the great ceremonial occasions in the Temple. Do we have here some confirmation of a priestly connection in the family?

All this is noteworthy but proves nothing. It is more important to assume that Jesus grew up in a home with brothers and sisters, aunts, uncles, cousins and grandparents. Some Christian traditions hold that Mary remained a virgin and that the names given of the brothers and sisters of Jesus were really those of cousins.[13] Whatever the case, the large extended family was a feature of Middle Eastern life. Jesus knew the cut and thrust as well as the joys of close family relationships.

Betrothal

Even the brief account of Mary and Joseph's courtship reveals real affection and respect. We

A Jewish bride dressed in traditional Yemenite costume. The modern Jewish wedding service consists of two parts: betrothal and marriage.

can be sure that Jesus grew up in a loving home. He also grew up in a home where the Jewish religious law was fully observed, as the birth stories show. The pre-marriage, betrothal agreement between Mary and Joseph is an example.[14]

Betrothal was not like a modern engagement. Although the couple did not live together, it was still so binding that it could only be terminated by divorce. The Oral Torah insisted on this point, basing itself firmly on the sanctity of marriage as taught in the Hebrew Bible.

Joseph, a religious man, was guided by the Oral Torah. When it seemed that Mary had betrayed him, he had no choice but to follow the accepted procedures and divorce her. He could not do this entirely secretly. The bill of divorce had to be handed to the woman, by the man or his proxy, before witnesses. Joseph therefore planned to do it as quietly as he could and then to use his influence to shield Mary from scandal.

A reminder of the former practice of betrothal exists to this day in the Jewish wedding service which is in two parts, betrothal and marriage. Once separated by a year, these two parts are now placed together.

Orthodox churches in the Middle East also go back to Jewish roots in a line barely influenced by western Christendom. They have a public betrothal service, solemnised by a priest, a year before the wedding. Although the agreement no longer needs a divorce to end it, a family is dreadfully disgraced if either party opts out of the anticipated marriage. Anyone living in a Christian Arab village will still see betrothal ceremonies but, with the encroaching influence of the West, the binding nature is now losing its force.

Circumcision and Naming

Circumcision is practised by many peoples but in Judaism it is the intimate sign of God's covenant with the Jewish people. For them, its origins go back to Abraham who lived some six hundred years before Moses received the Torah.[15] In familiar terminology it is called a *brit*, which is the Hebrew word for a covenant. Many Jewish people pronounce it as '*bris*', reflecting the customary pronunciation of older, eastern European, Jewish communities.

To this day, even non-religious Jews usually circumcise their sons. Boys are named at their *brit* while girls are named in the synagogue on the first Shabbat after their birth. Both John the Baptist and Jesus officially received their names at their circumcisions.[16]

In Hebrew, the name Jesus is Yeshua. Like the name Joshua, it comes from a root meaning salvation. Right at the beginning, the angel made it clear to Mary that her son was to have this name because he would save his people from their sins. This is significant in terms of the messianic expectations of the day when most people hoped for a political saviour who would free the nation from servitude to Rome.

Like most languages, Hebrew has its own peculiar swear words and curses. One such is the epithet *yeshu*, which is an acronym of the initial letters of three words—**Y**emach **SH**'mo **U**zichrono. They mean, 'May his name and memory be blotted out'. The curse is used chiefly to refer to anyone who has betrayed or brought shame upon Judaism, such as an apostate who has been excommunicated by the community.

The similarity between Yeshua and *yeshu* is obvious. Over the centuries, Jewish people have been so persecuted by so-called Christians and in the cause of Yeshua that they have learned to hate and fear his very name. (We cover this topic in a different context and slightly more fully in the last chapter of this book.) Little wonder, then, that the custom deliberately started of calling Jesus Yeshu instead of Yeshua.

Nowadays, many Jewish people know Jesus only as Yeshu. Most of them have no idea that this is incorrect and do not know what the term really means. They are genuinely upset if they find out.

Purification after Childbirth

In the story of Simeon, two biblical Jewish customs are intertwined; the purification of women after childbirth and the redemption of the firstborn son.[17] Some translations do not distinguish clearly between the two events, but when Mary and Joseph went to the Temple to offer her purification sacrifices, they also took the one-and-a-half-month-old Jesus to present him to the Lord for his redemption.

The injunctions concerning purification after childbirth are found in Leviticus 12. A woman was ritually unclean for a week after

Relatives gather around a baby boy for his circumcision (*bris*) at a Jerusalem synagogue.

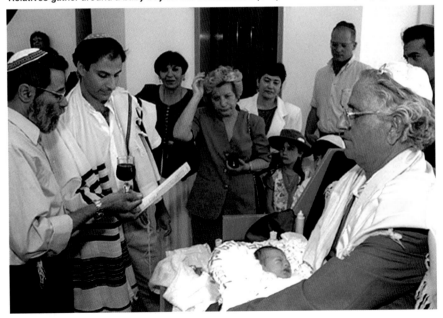

the birth of a boy and a fortnight for a girl. From then on she was technically clean provided there was no bleeding. Notwithstanding, she had to wait either thirty-three or sixty-six extra days before she could go through the process of ritual immersion and then make her sacrifices in the Temple. The rite of thanksgiving after childbirth, in both church and synagogue, originates here.

Note that the concept of ceremonial purity or impurity is not about hygiene but about fitness for religious activity. Ritual uncleanness barred both layman and priest from participating in Temple rituals. The later chapters in this book on religious customs and the Temple deal more fully with these things. Meanwhile, we piece together from the Mishnah the purification procedures which Mary must have followed.

The first thing she did was to immerse in the *mikveh,* which was a ritual bath. She then entered the Temple precincts and passed into the Court of the Women. There, certain horn shaped containers stood. Into a horn presided over by a priest and allocated for this purpose, she placed the money for her sacrifices. Only the priest knew if someone made the 'poor man's' offering and so no person was shamed before another. He kept a tally of what was paid for until, at a set time, the women gathered on a platform overlooking the altar in the priests' court beyond. There they watched the sacrifice of all the animals purchased for their sin and purification offerings.

Unto us a Son is Given

Many people wonder about the extra time allocated in Leviticus 12 for the purification

Cutaway illustration of a peasant's house from the time of Jesus.

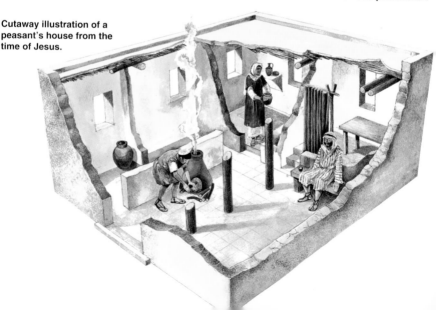

The hilltop town of Bethlehem lies just a few miles south of Jerusalem.

rituals after the birth of a girl. Does it merely reflect the male orientation of the culture of that time or does it imply a scriptural principle of male ascendancy over the female? As with many problems, the rabbis offer the most satisfying solution.

In Judaism there is a levitical principle that 'the life is in the blood'.[18] Any contact with death brings ritual impurity. The act of giving birth and the associated loss of blood is, therefore, a brush with death for both mother and child.

Seven days of ritual impurity for a boy follow from this encounter with death. The ensuing thirty-three days of specifically acknowledged ritual purity correspond to the fact that life has triumphed over death in the safe arrival of a baby. No further time is needed for a boy. For a girl, the first seven and the first thirty-three days are commemorated for the same reason; but something more is taken into consideration.

Each month a woman ovulates. If the ovum is not fertilised it dies and the woman menstruates. Every time this happens, she becomes unclean for seven days because of the moment of death that has taken place in her body.

When a girl is born, the same process will occur in her body once she is physically mature. A double time is therefore laid upon the mother to affirm her daughter's biological function. In this sense, the extra days celebrate the triumph of the life force within every woman. The Torah does not oppose feminism. It was not an issue in those days. Rather, it recognises the natural rhythms of a woman's body and the basic physiological difference between the sexes.

Redemption of the Firstborn

Once Mary was purified, she and Joseph could turn their attention to the Torah requirements

Possible Date of Jesus' Birth

1st of Nisan taken to equal 14 March

	Abijah's course on duty	Abijah's course ends duty	Approximate date in our calendar	Zechariah home for 4 days
If course served 2 weeks at a time	For weeks 15 and 16 of Jewish year	On day 112 of Jewish year	3 July	+4
If course served for 1 week twice a year	For week 8	On day 56	9 May	+4
	and week 32	and day 224	and 24 October	+4

enjoined upon their son. After the Passover deliverance of the firstborn from the angel of death, God chose all firstborn males for himself. This means that they were destined for religious duties on behalf of the nation.[19] He later transferred these duties exclusively to the tribe of Levi because its members had stood by Moses in the matter of the golden calf.[20]

Moses took a count of all Levite males and all other firstborn males over a month old. In an exact exchange, 273 firstborn had no Levites to take their place. They had to buy their freedom from God at five silver shekels apiece.[21] After that one-off event, the system demanded that every firstborn son, who was not from the tribe of Levi, be bought back or redeemed at one month old.

Parents took their son either to a local priest or to the Temple and paid the redemption price. As Bethlehem was near Jerusalem, Joseph and Mary delayed Jesus' redemption until the forty days had passed before Mary could be purified. They then combined the two events.

It is likely that Simeon was the priest who performed the redemption ceremony. Old priests who could no longer carry a full workload were allocated lighter duties. Simeon's blessing of Jesus is certainly coupled with the statement that his parents were doing 'what the Law required'.[22] This may well imply that Simeon was the officiating priest.

Many Jewish people still redeem their firstborn sons at thirty-one days old. The ceremony is of great antiquity. It is called *pidyon haben*, meaning the redemption of the son. Any man in the Jewish community who is surnamed Cohen (Hebrew for priest) is tradi-

Elizabeth conceives	6th Month of Elizabeth's pregnancy ends	Mary therefore conceives no later than	Length of pregnancy	Jesus born
7 July	after +168 days	28 December	+280 days	4 October
Either on 13 May	+168 days	Either 28 October	+280 days	Either 4 August
or on 28 October	+168 days	or 14 April	+280 days	or 19 January

tionally of priestly descent. Such a person is called upon to ask the parents if they will redeem their son or give him to God. Naturally, they opt for the former, pay him five silver coins which he usually donates to charity, and he declares the child redeemed.

There are jokes about parents who decide to leave their child unredeemed and in the care of Mr. Cohen, God's official priestly representative, until he stops crying at night or is potty trained. The rabbis have carefully defined who is the firstborn. Girls are never counted. The child who is eligible must not only be a woman's first son but also her first baby, the first to 'open the womb'. A first son but a second child does not count, nor does a boy after a miscarriage. A man has only one firstborn son who is eligible to be his heir but he can have a number of firstborn sons through different wives. For each of these he will perform the *pidyon haben* ceremony.

An interesting speculation now arises about Samuel. Did Hannah and Elkanah decide not to redeem him but to present him to God from infancy for a life of duty in the shrine at Shiloh? Or were they members of the tribe of Levi who simply sent their son into religious service at a much earlier age than was the norm?

Another query about a Levite can be answered here. At first reading, Elkanah is called an Ephraimite.[23] In a later genealogical list he is descended from Levi through Kohath.[24] The apparent contradiction can be explained. The Levites had no territorial inheritance and lived amongst all the tribes.[25] Therefore, a Levite living in Ephraim might casually be referred to as an Ephraimite.

Happy Birthday!

People have long wondered about the traditional date of Jesus' birth and made complicated calculations to work it out. One more recent theory suggests that he was born in the autumn, at the Feast of Tabernacles. It may be so, but nobody can be sure. The typology underlying this feast would certainly make it appropriate, for the coming of the messianic age has always been closely linked to Tabernacles, as the prophet Zechariah shows.[26]

This view is particularly popular amongst Messianic Jews, that is, Jewish people who believe in Jesus as their Lord, Saviour and Messiah. Quite a lot of Gentile Christians are also beginning to subscribe to it. Because of its growing popularity, we shall examine how the calculations are made.

Twenty-four different divisions of priests served in the Temple on a rota basis, as Chapters 11 and 16 of this book, on the Temple and Groups, explain. We know that Zechariah belonged to the course of Abijah[27], which was the eighth division on the duty rota.[28]

The Jewish religious year begins in spring with the month of Abib, or Nisan.[29] The first day of Nisan may fall anywhere in our March, or even in early April, depending on the appearance of the new moon. Like Easter, it varies each year. The attempt to prove that Jesus was born at Tabernacles starts by taking the 14th of March as a mid-way working date for the beginning of Nisan.

There are twelve lunar months of four weeks each in the regular Jewish year. Accepting that the term of service for each group of priests lasted for a fortnight, then the eighth division served during the fifteenth and sixteenth weeks of the year. Thus, the course of Abijah ended its duties on the hundred and twelfth day of the Jewish year. This is the 3rd of July as reckoned from the 14th of March.

Zechariah then returned home.[30] Luke does not say how soon it was before Elizabeth became pregnant but he implies that it was not long.[31] The proponents of the Tabernacles theory suggest that it was four days later, on July the 7th. The angel visited Mary when Elizabeth was in her sixth month of pregnancy.[32] Presumably these are lunar months of twenty-eight days each, in accordance with the Jewish calendar. If so, the Annunciation took place about twenty-four weeks or one hundred and sixty-eight days on in Elizabeth's pregnancy. Mary, therefore, conceived on the 28th of December.

Jesus was born forty weeks later, according to the usual length of a pregnancy. His birthday is thus deemed to fall on the 4th of October. Even if this assessment is only approximate, it is still reasonable to conclude from it that Jesus was born at, or close to, the Feast of Tabernacles.

Two Problems

There are two difficulties with this theory. The first problem is that it is calculated on the understanding that each priestly division served in the Temple for two weeks, once a year. It makes no concession to the fact that many commentators believe that the priests served for one week at a time and went up to Jerusalem twice a year.

The important thing to emphasise at this juncture is that we do not know. The relevant

The town of Nazareth is dominated today by the Basilica of the Annunciation. The Mount of Precipitation can be seen in the background.

passages in the Mishnah are ambiguous and no records exist to tell us exactly how the system worked. Because of the uncertainty, any valid attempt to ascertain the birth date of Jesus must look at the alternatives.

What happens if we assume that Abijah's course was on duty during the eighth week of the year and then again, for the thirty-second week? Let us continue to assume that the 1st of Nisan is the 14th of March. The course of Abijah now end its weeks of service fifty-six and two hundred and twenty-four days later respectively, on the 9th of May and the 24th of October.

On either occasion, Elizabeth might have conceived after Zechariah returned home. The probable dates of her conception are now the 13th of May or the 28th of October. The Annunciation to Mary, marking her conception, is on either the 28th of October or the 14th of April and Jesus is born on the 4th of

August or the 19th of January.

Neither date coincides with either the Feast of Tabernacles or Christmas. It is, however, surely of some significance that the January date, which could be much earlier, is reasonably close to the 6th of January, when Eastern Orthodox churches celebrate Christmas. Even more interesting is the fact that the Armenian church observes Christmas on the 19th of January. The roots of these churches are very ancient and we should never completely ignore old traditions.

The second problem relates to the number of months in the Jewish year. A normal lunar year has twelve months of four weeks each. In order for it to correlate with the solar calendar and for festivals to occur in the right seasons, adjustments are necessary. Five times, in a cycle of nineteen years, a leap month is added after the twelfth month.

In a regular forty-eight week cycle, the first

division would always take the first week (or two weeks) of Nisan and the twenty-fourth division would always close the cycle. What happened, however, every third or fourth year when a leap month was added? Did the rota simply follow its course? If so, the various sections would hardly ever be on duty for the same two weeks of the year. Alternatively, was there a method of working which ensured that the first division always covered the first week (weeks) of the first month?

We do not know. As with the gospels, the sources saw no need to explain such things to people who already knew them. Yet the question is far-reaching for us. If the courses did not always function on the same weeks of each year, then Zechariah could have been on duty at any time. Accordingly, there is no sure way of calculating the birthday of Jesus by this method or of proving that it was at Tabernacles.

Josephus tells us that the course of Jehoiarib was on duty when the Temple fell in 70 CE. This was the first course. The destruction of the Temple took place in summer, on the 9th of Av, the fifth month. If the first division always served at the start of the first month, and possibly at the start of the seventh, why was Jehoiarib's section at work in Av? True, this was a time of great crisis, but the priests always tried to keep the Temple running according to routine.

One other thing might have upset the rota system. The Mishnah describes how the course of Bilgah had lost its rights, either because it had been dilatory in its duties or because of inter-marriage with a heathen family. Another section stood in for it. We do not know the

details but, clearly, the arrangements did not always go to plan.

The conclusion surely is, at least in the opinion of this writer, that the Tabernacles' theory for Jesus' birth is doubtful. Still, because of the uncertainty of our knowledge, we do not dismiss it entirely.

John's gospel says something in this connection which is either very significant or a most expressive choice of vocabulary. 'The Word was made flesh, he lived among us'.[33] The Greek word translated as he 'lived among us', actually means he 'tabernacled' or 'pitched his tent' among us. By virtue of his intimate relationship with Jesus, did John know something about the time of his birth which caused him to use that particular expression? Once again, we do not know.

The 25th of December

The 25th of December closely marks the mid-winter solstice in the northern hemisphere. This was always a time of festivity to welcome the lengthening days and return of the sun. In the Roman Empire, the celebrations were held in honour of the god Saturn and were known as the Saturnalia.

It appears that the Christians of the Roman world, feeling unhappy with the pagan calendar, decided to substitute their own festival for the Saturnalia. The event that they chose to celebrate was Jesus' birthday, Christmas. In this way, they too could rejoice and enjoy the holiday mood at the same time as their non-Christian neighbours.

Why did they decide to remember the birth of Jesus and not some other happening in his life? Was it because they knew of a tradition which placed his birth close to this time of year? They must have had some good reason for their choice. In the absence of any definite evidence, we can only reiterate that we do not know.

Type and Symbol

Whatever the date of Jesus' birth and whatever the details of his upbringing, there is no doubt that he lived in a godly home and that Mary and Joseph reared him according to the precepts of the Torah. It is helpful to see how these ancient ceremonies of the law, which we have examined in this chapter, enshrine spiritual truths and are thereby types of spiritual realities and experiences.

For instance, God's people must be betrothed to him in holiness and truth.[34] There is a circumcision of the heart as well as of the body.[35] Jesus is the firstborn of creation,[36] the firstborn of many brethren and the firstborn from the dead.[37] Ritual immersion and sacrifice cannot make a person righteous before God. Only the cleansing power of the blood of Jesus can deal with sin.[38]

Bible references

1 Matthew 1:1–17
2 Luke 3:23–38
3 2 Kings 23:31—25:30;
   2 Chronicles 36
4 Matthew 1:12,16
5 Jeremiah 22:30
6 1 Chronicles 3:17–19;
   Nehemiah 12:1
7 1 Chronicles 3:5;
   Luke 3:31
8 Matthew 1:12
9 Luke 3:27
10 Luke 1:36
11 Luke 1:5

12 John 18:15,16
13 Mark 6:3
14 Matthew 1:18–25
15 Genesis 17:9–14, 21:4
16 Luke 1:59, 2:21
17 Luke 2:22–35
18 Leviticus 17:11,14
19 Exodus 13:11–16
20 Exodus 32:25–29;
   Numbers 3:11–13
21 Numbers 3:39–51
22 Luke 2:27
23 1 Samuel 1:1
24 1 Chronicles 6:16–28
25 Deuteronomy 18:1, 2
26 Zechariah 14:16–19

27 Luke 1:5
28 1 Chronicles 24:10
29 Exodus 12:1,2
30 Luke 1:23
31 Luke 1:24
32 Luke 1:36
33 John 1:14
34 Luke 1:26;
   Hosea 2:19,20 RSV
35 Deuteronomy 10:16, 30:6;
   Colossians 2:11
36 Romans 8:29 RSV
37 Colossians 1:15,18
38 Hebrews 9:9–14, 10:19–22

CHAPTER THREE

The Education Jesus Received

The religious leaders in Judaea tended to feel, as the Gospels show, that Jesus and his disciples were ignorant and uneducated because they came from Galilee and had never studied.[1] By this they meant that they had never studied the Torah under one of their own teachers of the Law. The reason for this attitude was partly rooted in a certain prejudice which regarded Judaea, centred upon Jerusalem, as superior to Galilee. Could Jesus possibly have received a proper religious education in Galilee?

The Ignorant Galileans

The Jerusalem Temple, the very soul of Jewish religious and national existence, was in Judaea. In turn, Judaea was the centre of orthodoxy and leadership. Yet, in many ways, Judaeans were insular. They did not like mixing with foreigners and had as little contact with them as possible. It was just as well that the trade routes merely skirted their mountainous terrain and that the stony valleys amongst the hills did not encourage foreign settlers. True, pilgrims from all parts of the world converged on Jerusalem for the three annual feasts of Judaism, but they were fellow Jews or converts to Judaism and not Gentile aliens.

By contrast, Galilee was so diversely populated that it was often known as Galilee of the Gentiles. Josephus tells of two hundred and forty prosperous towns in the region, mostly with mixed Jewish and Gentile populations. Agriculture and trades flourished. Important trade routes intersected the area. The Romans built paved roads in all their dominions to facilitate the movement of their armies. Numerous services, including inns and brothels, supplied the needs of traders, soldiers and travellers from distant lands.

As a result, Galilean Jews were more exposed to other cultures and values. This, in turn, may have led to a more mature relationship with Gentiles than that evidenced by Judaean Jews. It may equally have resulted in a compromising of their distinct religious identity. Some sources present them as devout but in a simpler, less casuistic way than the Judaeans. Other sources vilify them for having diluted their faith for the sake of peace with their neighbours.

At the same time, Galilee was also a centre for the Zealots. Their fiery Jewish nationalism eventually played its part in determining the history of the whole nation. Was this a reaction of some to what they saw as the worldliness of their fellow Jews there in Galilee?

The town of Nazareth was part of the network. Nazareth did not have a good name. In part this was because it was on a major trade route going inland from the coast and was, thereby, closely in touch with the Gentile world. One thing stood in its favour. It was a local gathering point for the priests who met to travel up to Jerusalem together for their twice yearly spells of duty in the Temple. The

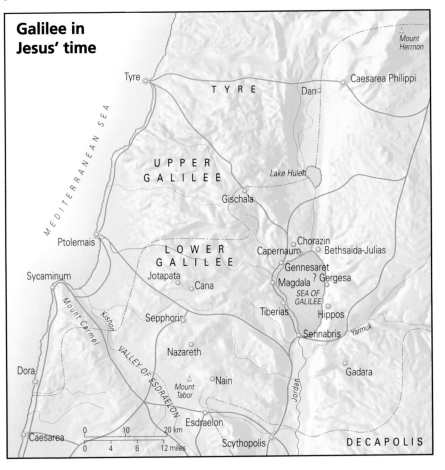

Galilee in Jesus' time

system is explained in Chapter 11 (page 117).

What we must deduce from all this is that Jesus was no backwoods boy, ignorant of the ways of the world. He could not live in Galilee, much less Nazareth, and isolate himself entirely from contact with Gentile life. For a young boy, lots of exciting things were constantly happening in Nazareth. Jesus could not help but grow up as a young man experienced in living as part of a cosmopolitan society.

At Home

There is a Jewish saying that 'a child sucks in knowledge of the Torah at the mother's breast'. In other words, education begins in infancy. Mary and Joseph clearly lived according to the Jewish religious law. From his earliest days, therefore, Jesus must have watched his mother prepare for the Sabbath and kindle the festal lights according to a custom which was already some centuries old even then. The Mishnah traces its inception to pre-Maccabean times. It discusses the kind of oil and wick used for the light which was, of course, a clay oil lamp and not a wax candle.

Every Sabbath Jesus would have heard Mary say words which are not far different, if at all, from the words which Jewish mothers still say every Friday evening: 'Blessed art Thou, O Lord our God, King of the Universe, who hast sanctified us by His commands and hast commanded us to kindle the Sabbath lights'.

The Sabbath continues with the *Kiddush*. This is a blessing over a glass of wine which sanctifies all joyous Jewish occasions. The

A kindergarten Torah class learn Hebrew.

word comes from a Hebrew root *k-d-sh*, meaning to sanctify or set apart. Traditionally, *Kiddush* goes back to the Men of the Great Assembly. They were teachers of the Torah who lived in the time after Ezra and led the people in godly ways.

As head of the home, Joseph must have poured wine for his family each Friday evening and taught his sons to say this, or a very similar prayer: 'Blessed art Thou, O Lord our God, King of the Universe, Creator of the fruit of the vine'. If, as is likely, he died early, then the duty of making *Kiddush* would have devolved upon Jesus, the eldest son of the family.

The Gospels record how all Jesus' family were known in the local synagogue which they obviously attended regularly each Sabbath. The whole day, which began at sunset on Friday and ended at sunset on Saturday, was given over to worship and relaxation. However pressing the financial need or however urgent an order, the carpenter's shop in Nazareth closed down on this day for work on the

Sabbath was forbidden by Jewish law. So strictly defined and observed were the Sabbath rules that even to search one's clothes for a flea was accounted work!

Sabbath closes with *Havdalah,* a ceremony separating the especially sacred day from the ordinary working days. This institution is also ascribed in Jewish tradition to the so-called Men of the Great Assembly. At the end of a festive meal and as the sun was setting, the family shared a final cup of wine, and lights and incense were brought in to the accompaniment of appropriate blessings. Jewish people still use wine today and light a twisted, multi-wicked candle and smell sweet spices. A short, beautiful prayer then concluded the Sabbath.

All children enjoy watching their mother bake and being allowed to help. It was a housewife's daily chore to grind flour and make enough bread to last the family for the day. Did Jesus ever ask his mother about the small lump of dough which she always set aside in obedience to the Law when she mixed the daily portion for her growing brood?[2] This token offering to God, which orthodox Jews still make, sanctified the whole batch of common bread and reminded people of their dependence on God for their food every day.

Paul draws upon the same, homely, domestic act to reinforce the picture of the olive tree which he used to illustrate the profound truth of Israel's eternal standing before

Jewish boys learn from the rabbi how to read the Hebrew scriptures.

God.[3] Even if some individual members of the people of Israel fall short of God's standards, the nation as a whole still has a role to play in his purposes.

Perhaps from his father Jesus learned the reason for the *mezuzah* on the doorpost and copied him in touching it as he went in and out of his home. A *mezuzah* is a small piece of parchment held in a decorated container and inscribed with Deuteronomy 6:4–9 and 11:13–21. It constantly reminded the people that they were to hold God's teaching in the heart, head and home.[4] A *mezuzah* literally fulfils the command to write God's law on the doorposts of the home. It is affixed at an angle to the right hand door jamb and shows to this day that a Jewish family lives in a house.

Jewish fathers also taught their sons how to put on the *phylacteries* or prayer boxes which were used on special religious occasions. Worn on the head and left arm, they fulfilled the command to write God's law on the head and heart.

Simple matters of ritual cleanliness were also learned in the home, such as how to wash the hands before food and to say the accompanying prayer: 'Blessed art Thou, O Lord our God, King of the Universe, who hast sanctified us with His commandments and hast commanded us concerning the washing of the hands'. Grace before food was another duty: 'Blessed art Thou, O Lord our God, King of the Universe, who bringest forth bread from the earth'.

Practically all the above customs are examined in other chapters in this book. Whatever man-made regulations had developed around these practices under the Oral Torah, they were all familiar routines in every observant,

Ritual handwashing. Handwashing before food was taught at home.

Jewish home. The rituals and prayers which Jesus followed are, in essence, still the same today. Since their inception they have always been part of a Jewish child's education and they have always bound Jewish families closely together.

The Educational System

According to rabbinic tradition, a Jewish father was bound to teach his son as soon as the boy could speak. The duty took precedence even over eating a meal. The child learned short Psalms and Scripture verses, wise sayings of the sages and simple prayers such as are quoted above. Great store was laid on accuracy of memory because the ancient world had no printed material, only that which was written by hand.

Already by the time of the Maccabees, over a century before Jesus, many Jewish homes possessed scrolls containing parts of the Scriptures and scrolls with specially selected portions for children. This implies a good standard of literacy and commitment to learning even in those days, in spite of the

there was no school. Every community with twenty-five suitable boys was bound to appoint a schoolmaster. For more than forty he had to have an assistant. Above fifty boys warranted a second master. The school was attached to the synagogue and the teacher was a synagogue official but classes might well be held outdoors in some quiet, shady spot. The pupils sat on the ground in a semi-circle around the teacher.

The Mishnah contains an informative ethical treatise called *Pirqei Abot* or Ethics of the Fathers. Abot records sayings and customs which reflect a way of life already widely established well before the time when they were committed to writing. One passage classifies the ages and subjects of study for a Jewish boy. 'At five one reaches the age for the study of Scripture, at ten the study of the Mishnah'. Secular subjects had no place in the curriculum. Moral and religious learning was the only aim. What did this involve?

The commonly spoken language of the region, even for Jewish people, was Aramaic. Hebrew was still a living language, familiar to most Jews and used in all religious functions. The sacred texts which were studied were in Hebrew. A five-year-old boy may well have learned his Hebrew alphabet at home and been able to read and write easy words before he went to school. If so, all to the good! His first textbook was Leviticus.

Leviticus is one of the hardest books in the Bible for many western Christians but for that culture it was a good choice. The customs and laws it describes were part of a child's daily life in the home and in the workplace. A highlight of any child's experience was to go to Jerusalem with his father and male relatives to

A *mezuzah* is placed ceremonially on a new Jerusalem synagogue

fact that a more formal approach to learning only came later.

Two sages are credited with encouraging education of the young. Some seventy years before Jesus, Shimon ben Shetach opened schools and laid the foundations of a good elementary system. Joshua of Gamala in Galilee, who was martyred under Herod the Great, then introduced schools into every town. He actively advocated compulsory education for all Jewish boys from the age of five or six.

Rabbinic traditions further tell us that, from a religious point of view, it soon was deemed unlawful for a family to live in a place where

observe one of the festivals in the Temple and to offer sacrifices and tithes. This was a wonderful opportunity to see for himself the practical outworking of the things which he had learned about in Leviticus.

Round about ten years of age, a boy began to study the oral traditions surrounding the written Torah. In Jesus' day there were no textbooks for this study as none of the vast body of oral lore was as then written down. It was preserved in the minds of scholars who made it their lives' work to study and memorise its every detail. They taught it to their followers who in turn passed it down to others.

The expertise of a village schoolmaster was often limited but it was sufficient. Most children gave up before very long, either because they were not academically able or they had to work to help keep the family. A clever boy was encouraged to continue studying and to seek instruction from one of the more famous teachers of the day. These were mostly in Jerusalem, but even a village schoolmaster might prove his worth with an apt pupil.

Spiritual and Intellectual Excellence

Jesus went to Jerusalem for the Passover when he was twelve years old.[5] His parents went up every year but we do not know if this was the first time for Jesus or not. Women were not required to go up by the religious law as were the men, but it seems that a crowd of relatives and friends customarily travelled together and made a lively holiday of the pilgrimage.

Did Jesus have his *Bar Mitzvah* on this occasion? Strictly speaking the answer is presumably, no. *Bar Mitzvah*, meaning son of the commandment, is today a coming of age

A large mezuzah at Jerusalem's Jaffa Gate.

ceremony when thirteen-year-old boys become responsible for their own religious lives. Some early rabbis used the term but the ceremony itself is only mentioned in the fifteenth century CE.

We do know that almost all societies pinpoint some age when their children officially enter into responsible adulthood. We cannot rule out the possibility that twelve was a significant age for Jewish boys in those days. A trip to Jerusalem would have been a very suitable way of signifying that a boy was entering into manhood, with all the responsibilities thereby entailed. Was this the implication of that visit to Jerusalem?

The fact that Jesus, at twelve years old, astounded the greatest scholars of his day is the strongest argument for his having had a good early education. We might ask, what about his own, innate ability? Doubtless, he must have had this too. At the same time, it is questionable whether he could have dealt with the scholars in such a way as to impress them so greatly if he had not been taught something of their viewpoints and methods.

When Jesus discussed matters of the Torah with the rabbis in the Temple, it was no ordinary occasion. During the major festivals, Jews came to Jerusalem from all over the known world. The most famous and erudite rabbis customarily held 'master classes' in religious law in the Temple courtyards for the benefit of the visitors. Anyone could join the discussion and question or challenge the teachers. Of course, to do so convincingly one needed a high standard of learning. This Jesus obviously had.

How could his parents, who paid the poor man's offering for Mary's purification,[6] afford to let him study sufficiently to reach such a high standard of academic excellence, especially with a growing family? One answer might be that they used the valuable gifts of the wise men to supplement the family income and free Jesus for extra tuition. Perhaps he learned quickly and did not need an undue amount of study time. Nor was the school system comparable with our own.

The Carpenter and Son of a Carpenter

Jewish boys, even from well-to-do families, all learned a trade. Jesus did not study all the time. As he grew up he was also expected to acquire his father's carpentry skills. At this juncture we pause. Having made the commonly accepted assumption that Joseph was a carpenter, some readers may be dismayed to learn that certain commentators question it.

In both Greek and Hebrew, the words most regularly translated as carpenter simply mean

An artist's impression of two carpenters at work in the time of Jesus.

an artificer or craftsman who might work in stone or metal as well as wood. This is true of the Greek word used in the Gospels which is taken to mean that Jesus and his father were both carpenters. It is just possible that they were craftsmen who worked in a variety of materials. Wood was probably more scarce and expensive in those days than we realise.

Some Jewish scholars, who have undertaken to study the life of Jesus, offer a yet more radical suggestion. The Talmud uses the idiom, 'carpenter and son of a carpenter', to refer to a wise and learned man. They are not sure whether a proverb cited in the Talmud was known some three or four hundred years earlier in the time of Jesus. They do know that many folk sayings often go back into antiquity. If this maxim does so, then the references to Jesus' trade in the story of the synagogue[7] in Nazareth might be open to a different interpretation.

Those who propound this view feel that the Gospel writers were faced with a linguistic problem when they described the event. Did the members of the congregation express their amazement at Jesus' great erudition by quoting a familiar, Hebrew saying, 'carpenter and son of a carpenter'? In the subsequent translation into Greek, was the use of the term carpenter confused, thus leading to the generally approved understanding that Jesus and his father were workers in wood?

Probably most of us feel unwilling to abandon the beloved image of Jesus at the carpenter's bench. In spite of our preferences, we should guard against closing our minds to new ideas or rejecting them for no better reason than that we do not care for them.

Whatever the case, the tradition was that no one should make a living from study of the Torah or from teaching it. The pursuit of Torah was motivated by love and was to be a joy in and for itself. Therefore, the early rabbis all had daily jobs by which they earned their keep. We know of rabbis by name who were farmers, street sweepers, shop keepers and other. Paul, too, paid his own way in life by making and mending tents.[8]

In practical terms, if Joseph died while the family was young, Jesus, as the eldest, would have worked hard to help Mary bring up the smaller children. He may even have helped to train his younger brothers in the skills of his own trade. This might explain why he was in his late twenties before he left home to begin his ministry.

Thus, the picture emerges of a child growing up in a cosmopolitan environment yet shielded from the vices of the Gentile world; intellectually able but an ordinary carpenter; knowing the security of a loving home while sharing the harder experiences of the human lot. Jesus was so entirely a child of his times that we cannot fully know him without studying the environment which conditioned him.

Bible references	6 Luke 2:25
	Leviticus 5:7
1 John 7:15, 52	7 Matthew 13:55
2 Numbers 15:19–21	Mark 6:3
3 Romans 11:16–18	8 Acts 18:1–3
4 Deuteronomy 6:4–9	
5 Luke 2:41–50	

CHAPTER FOUR

The Clothes Jesus Wore

As far as we know, Jesus and his disciples were working class, country people, with two exceptions—Matthew who was a professional tax man and Judas Iscariot, whose very surname, *ish keriot* in Hebrew, implies a townsman. In contrast, the women who followed Jesus and supported his itinerant ministry must have been well off. At least one was a lady of class and she was Joanna, the wife of Herod's steward.[1]

Whether a person was rich or poor; town, village or desert dweller; professional or working class; the clothes worn were similar with just a few distinguishing variations in style and quality. Because fashions rarely change in the Middle East, we have some idea of how things used to be. This is borne out by comparing clothes described in the Bible with the garments worn early in this century, and even today in some places. It is only in the latter half of the last century that western fashions began to take over.

Robes and Belts

The basic garment was a flowing, ankle length robe with long, loose sleeves and tied with a girdle or belt. The material was hand woven from cotton for the poor and from silk for the wealthy. The cloth was often used

Typical man's clothing from the time of Jesus.

women both wore robes of only slightly differing cut and shape.

Girdles or belts were fashioned from wool, silk or leather. The purse referred to by Jesus was a pouch inside the belt which safely held small coins and valuables.[2] For active work, the robe is caught up in front and twisted into the belt to expose and free the legs for movement. The Bible calls this 'girding the loins'.

The Israelites left Egypt with girded loins, thus enabling them to hurry and man-handle their luggage.[3] Elijah ran before Ahab with girded loins.[4] The almost impossibly ideal wife of Proverbs girds up her loins to work beside her servants.[5] Jesus uses the same image to warn against spiritual slacking.[6] Peter exhorts his readers to gird up their minds, ready for mental action in the Christian life.[7]

The wide sleeves of the gown were shaped to a point which hung below the fingers. To free the arms for work they were pulled up above the elbow and the tapered ends tied together in front of the chest. The joined sleeves were then thrown back over the head so that the knotted part lay across the back of the shoulders. Being so long and full, this was not uncomfortable and it left the arms unhampered for whatever tasks there were to perform. As with the loins, to 'bare one's arm' means to be ready for action. When the Lord 'bares his holy arm' it is a sign that he is about to act on Israel's behalf.[8]

Jacob gave Joseph a coat of many colours or, as some translations like the Jerusalem Bible say, a robe with sleeves.[9] A wealthy man's heir might wear a robe with sleeves too voluminous to be tied back for manual work. In some Bedouin tribes only the chief and his heir wear such garments. However, we also

Woman's clothing and child's clothing from the time of Jesus.

in its undyed, natural state or bleached white. If colours were preferred, they used vegetable dyes to give the deep blues and indigo which are still seen today. Men and

der the older brothers were angry.

Cloaks and Camel Hair

The cloak was made from two lengths of material stitched together down the vertical edge. The approximate square thus formed was opened out so that the seam lay horizontally across the middle. The left and right sides were folded over to meet down the centre to become the front of the cloak. Both front and back parts were sewn together at the top to shape the neck and shoulders. Bound side slits sufficed for the armholes. All classes of people wore cloaks but for the poor they were essential items of clothing whereas a rich man's cloak might be of more decorative than practical use.

The best cloaks were woven from goat or camel hair and were coarse but warm and waterproof. John the Baptist wore camel hair and a leather belt and ate 'locusts and wild honey'.[10] This does not mean that he wore skins like Tarzan but rather that he dressed and lived as a peasant, even though his father was a priest. He wore a woven camel-hair cloak and the working man's leather girdle.

The word usually translated as locust probably referred to something entirely different from the grasshopper-like insect. Many commentators think that it was the common carob pod. The carob pod is brown, flat and hard and about seven inches long and one wide. The small seeds inside gave the name 'carat' to the weight measurement of gold and jewels. It grows on a low tree and, being wild and plentiful, the poor gathered it for food. The pod is very nutritious. People today who cannot take cocoa products sometimes substitute carob flour instead.

A rich man's clothing from the time of Jesus.

know from Egyptian tomb paintings that semitic chiefs of patriarchal times wore brightly coloured robes as an insignia of rulership. Either way, Jacob's gift marked his second youngest son as his chosen heir. No won-

Neither was wild honey necessarily bee honey. The only explicit biblical reference to bee honey is in the story of Samson.[11] The Hebrew word *davash* was more commonly used for any syrup or nectar extracted from fruit, and especially from the date. Carobs and dates were most likely John's staple diet.

Though not worn in hot weather, cloaks were used as bed coverings even in summer in desert areas and on higher ground where the nights are cold. Many poor people, therefore, needed them all year round. This is why the Torah forbids keeping a pledged cloak overnight, otherwise, 'what would a poor person have to sleep in?'[12]

Living in the Judaean desert, as he did, where the days were hot but the nights decidedly cold, John the Baptist's cloak was important to him. The fact that it was made of camel hair also tells us that he had a warm covering whenever he had occasion to sleep out in the open.

The soldiers cast lots for Jesus' cloak which was valuable because it was seamless.[13] It is interesting that only John records this fact, for apparently he was the one disciple who stayed to the very end with Jesus on the cross.

We know that in north Galilee there were large looms capable of producing a double width of material, wide enough for weaving the less commonly found seamless cloaks. Being more rare, they were also more expensive. How come that Jesus, a Galilean but not a rich man, wore such a garment? Did Mary or some close relative own one of the large looms and weave him the cloak as a gift?

A Palestinian woman's headcovering.

Heads and Feet

Most people had a head covering as a protection from the strong sun. Villagers and townsmen favoured turbans. Nomadic desert dwellers used a flowing scarf held in place with a cord. They pulled it entirely across the face in a sandstorm.

Women wore a close fitting cap which they covered with a veil. This was not a short, gauzy affair but a sturdy piece of material some six foot square. Doubled into a triangle and thrown over the head, not the face, it hung across the shoulders and down the back. Obviously it was removed for working. It also made a useful bag. Boaz asked Ruth to bring her veil and put six measures of barley in it for her to take home to her mother-in-law.[14] This was about fifteen litres dry measurement of grain.

Although everyone dressed more or less alike according to social standing, each village had some distinguishing feature. Bethlehem women wore a conical cap. When they married, their husband gave them a number of silver coins which they fixed to their hat. The coins were their security, only to be used in drastic circumstances or if the husband died. When he wanted a telling illustration, did Jesus recall how his mother once lost one of her coins and turned the house upside down until she found it?[15]

Country and poor folk often went barefoot. Townspeople might wear leather shoes but in a hot climate, sandals were most comfortable. Sandals have been preserved in burial chambers so we know what they were like. A long strap, attached at one end to a leather sole, was wound around the foot and ankle and secured to the sole again. The angel who freed Peter from prison told him to 'bind on' his sandals. This is a better translation than 'put on' for it preserves the idea of how the strap functioned.[16]

Everywhere the ground was stony and rough. Even today, if you walk on a dirt track during summer you will stir up a choking cloud of dust. On the same path in winter you squelch in ankle deep mud. The first priority when you get home is to wash your feet and sandals or rinse your boots. Foot washing in Bible times was part of cleanliness and comfort. Only in this context do we see how deliberately and deeply Simon the Pharisee insulted Jesus by failing to wash his feet when he invited him into his house as a guest.[17]

Beauty and Adornment

Palestinian women today wear beautifully embroidered dresses. You know a woman's village by the embroidery pattern and colour of her dress. For example, women from Ramallah wear creamy, white robes patterned with a rich red embroidery. Young girls learn to sew and are expected to make their own trousseau and items for their future home. Only in recent times have they started to use machines and buy some of the items.

Such is the strength of tradition that we can well imagine how the women who associated with Jesus also made and embellished their clothes. Embroidery was a skill in Bible times. The tabernacle contained curtains embroidered in blue, red and purple.[18] Deborah imagines how Sisera's mother, unaware of his defeat in battle, explains his delay by thinking of him dividing up the booty, amongst which were dyed and embroidered garments.[19]

Leather sandals Jesus would have worn.

Jewellery, perfume, make up and fancy hair styles were all part of a woman's life. Archaeologists have discovered necklaces, earrings, nose rings, bangles and much more made from gold and precious stones. They have analysed the dried-up contents of perfume bottles and cosmetic jars. Wall carvings and mosaics show these things, including elaborate hair fashions. In both the Old and the New Testaments lavish adornment was assumed to be a sign of pride.[20]

Festal Garments

The Scriptures often mention festal garments. It appears that they were robes designed to be worn on special occasions or a wealthy person gave them as a gift to those he wished to honour.

Abraham's servant presented jewels and raiment to Rebekah's family when he arranged her betrothal to Isaac.[21] Joseph made his brothers such a present when they were reconciled to him in Egypt. Significantly, he gave Benjamin, his full brother, five pieces of raiment instead of one.[22] Naaman took gold and ten festal robes as a present for the king of Israel if he could cure his leprosy.[23]

Jesus told the story of a man at a wedding who declined to wear the wedding garment which the host customarily provided for all the guests. He then drew a spiritual lesson from the incident which seems to be that we must be clothed, metaphorically, with the robe of righteousness in order to enter the kingdom of Heaven.[24] In the book of Revelation, members of the Sardis church who were victorious in their struggle against sin were to receive new, white robes.[25]

It is interesting that the custom of giving festal garments has persisted into recent times. There are records of nineteenth century travellers to various Middle Eastern countries who received audience with local potentates. To honour them, the rulers gave them ornately decorated robes. One gentleman described in his journal how he often received such gifts from a certain *pasha*. He soon discovered that it was the expected practice to sell the garments to a dealer in the *suk* or market. The merchant then resold them to the *pasha*, and thus they made a perpetual round.

Worn for Religious Purposes

Anyone attending an orthodox synagogue today will see that the men are all wearing prayer shawls. These are large squares of cream material bordered with black stripes and with long tassels at the four corners. They throw them around the shoulders and flick up the sides to form a kind of cape. In progressive synagogues the prayer shawl is a narrow stole but it still has the important feature, namely, four tassels.

The history of this garment, if such it can be called, goes back to Moses. Because of one man's disobedience, God commanded the people to put fringes with a thread of blue on their clothes to remind them that they must obey his law.[26] From this injunction and through various stages of development comes the modern prayer shawl or *tallit* worn by Jewish people in the synagogue today.

A mannequin dressed in the bridal costume of a Palestinian tribe.

Traditionally, the dye for the blue thread came from a rare sea mollusc which made it expensive. Lydia, one of Paul's converts in Philippi, was in the purple dye trade which may have been the same business.[27] No blue is used in the tassel nowadays as the exact shade is not known.

Indigo dye was cheaper and it was hard to tell the difference but the authorities condemned its use. Quite recently some Israeli archaeologists found prayer shawls belonging to the soldiers of Bar Cochba who led a rebellion against Rome in 131–135 CE. They were surprised to discover, on analysis, that the dye was indigo.

We are not sure how the tassel was made in Jesus' day. Today it consists of four long strands threaded through each corner hole and then doubled over to make eight. One strand is longer than the others. It is wound thirty-nine times around the remaining seven with five knots interspersed at equal intervals. All this is symbolic.

Thirty-nine stands for the books of the Jewish Bible, known to Christians as the Old Testament. Five symbolises the books of the Torah. The Hebrew word for a tassel is *tzitzit*. As all Hebrew letters have a numerical value, those of the word *tzitzit* add up to six hundred. This plus the eight threads and five knots makes six hundred and thirteen, the traditional number of commandments in the Torah. Modern Judaism delights in calculations of such complexity.

In New Testament times, ordinary people only wore a *tallit* on special occasions, if at all. It was the Pharisees who seem to have worn it regularly and, apparently in some cases, often for show. Jesus expresses no disapproval of the custom itself but he does condemn the extra long fringes which they affected to display their piety.[28] Despite this, he must sometimes have worn one himself as the story of the woman who touched the hem of his garment suggests.[29] Were they the ritual tassels that she touched? Other people, too, were healed by touching the borders or tassels of his clothes.[30]

Phylacteries are not articles of clothing but they have a similar purpose to the prayer shawl and they are, so to speak, worn. The Torah ordained that God's words and deeds on Israel's behalf are to be kept in the consciousness like a sign on the hand or between the eyes.[31] Israel took the injunction literally and created two

Palestinian women wear decorated costumes.

A Jewish man's prayer shawl.

ing peculiar to that language alone. Any approximating Greek term was almost bound to have some idolatrous connotations. An alternative approach might have been to incorporate the Hebrew word into the Greek text. In that case, Gentile readers who were unfamiliar with Jewish customs would not have known what was meant.

Phylacteries, or *tephillin*, are still worn during prayer today. As with long tassels, Jesus deplored ostentatiously large phylacteries as being a hypocritical show of piety.[28] Whether he himself ever wore them is a matter for conjecture, but it is likely.

Clothes Make the Man!

We are all familiar with pictures of the fair haired, blue eyed Jesus in idyllic surroundings. Famous paintings in art galleries show a richly adorned, renaissance figure set against a distinctly Italianate background. So relevant is he to every age and culture that artists happily create him in the image of their own world. African artists paint him black, and why not? But what did he really look like? Obviously, no one can say, although there may be hints in the relics of the ancient world.

For example, skeletons found in old burial chambers indicate that people were generally smaller than they are now. Pictures carved on ruined monuments in places like Egypt or Assyria show events in the lives of important rulers. From these, with their accompanying hieroglyphic or cuneiform inscriptions, archaeologists can recognise different racial types.

The facial features of the semitic peoples are fine and, contrary to the often held image, the nose is long, slim and pointed rather than

small boxes, each containing four passages of Scripture from Exodus 13:1–10, 13:11–16, Deuteronomy 6:4–9 and 11:13–21. One they strapped around the forehead and the other on the left arm whenever they said their prayers.

In first century Greek, the word 'phylactery' actually means a charm or amulet which had power to protect its wearer from malign spirits and influences. In Hebrew they are called *tephillin* and are thus linked to the word *tephillah*, a prayer.

Here is an example of how difficult it often is to find an exact Greek translation for a Hebrew word which has a very specific mean-

large and hooked. This latter is a Hittite characteristic and not a semitic one. The caricature has persisted to this day but it is incorrect, as a walk through the streets of any city in modern Israel would indicate.

Although we must emphasise the impreciseness of the following descriptions, they are worth drawing attention to because they do add a further dimension to the picture we are trying to create. Certain carvings show that people taken to be Israelites or semitic types had fairly short beards, tidily trimmed and gently pointed. Their hair was dark and of medium length, cut just above the shoulders and brushed back to reveal the ears. It is not tightly curled like the Assyrians nor squared off round the head like the Egyptians. It lies flat on top of the head then fluffs out behind the neck in a bouffant style.

Esau may have had red hair according to the account of his birth.[32] A Jewish tradition holds that the reference to David being ruddy means the same.[33] It could be so, but when he fled from Saul, his wife put a household idol in his bed to deceive the soldiers. She used a piece of goat skin to imitate his hair.[34] Black goats are everywhere in the land, but has anyone ever seen a red one? Just occasionally, however, you do see a goat with a russet tinge.

Perhaps some people did have reddish coloured hair in those days. If so, it was unusual enough to draw attention to it and it is unlikely that Jesus had this physical characteristic. Be that as it may, people who belong to the Middle East are usually swarthy skinned, dark haired and brown eyed. The blue eyes which one sometimes sees amongst the indigenous Arabs today are said to be a Crusader relic.

Phylacteries can be seen on the foreheads of both man and boy at this *Barmitzvah*.

In view of all this, might we reasonably wonder whether Jesus looked more like some of the old wall carvings than the impressions of him painted by numerous artists down the years? We do know that what he was did not depend on what he wore but on his relationship with God. We also know that a godly person, despite lines of pain and age, will have an inner attraction which marks the face. That this was true of Jesus, the gospel story leaves us in no doubt, as it describes the way in which people from every walk of life responded to him.

Bible references

1 Luke 8:2,3
2 Luke 10:4
3 Exodus 12:11 RSV
4 1 Kings 18:46 RSV
5 Proverbs 31:17 RSV
6 Luke 12:35
7 1 Peter 1:13; Isaiah 52:10
9 Genesis 37:3, Jerusalem Bible; 'sleeves', KJV
10 Mark 1:6
11 Judges 14:8
12 Exodus 22:26, 27 Good News Bible
13 John 19:23 KJV
14 Ruth 3:15 KJV
15 Luke 15:8
16 Acts 12:8 KJV
17 Luke 7:44
18 Exodus 35:35
19 Judges 5:30
20 Isaiah 3:18–24; 1 Timothy 2:9
21 Genesis 24:53
22 Genesis 45:22
23 2 Kings 5:5
24 Matthew 22:11
25 Revelation 3:5
26 Numbers 15:32–41
27 Acts 16:14
28 Matthew 23:5
29 Luke 8:43, 44
30 Mark 6:56
31 Deuteronomy 6:4–9
32 Genesis 25:25
33 1 Samuel 16:12 RSV
34 1 Samuel 19:11–17

CHAPTER FIVE

The Language Jesus Spoke

A Multilingual Society

Before the Assyrian and Babylonian captivities, the language of the inhabitants of Israel and Judah was Hebrew. Once in Babylon, the Judaean exiles had to learn the local tongue. This was Aramaic, which was a semitic language closely related to Hebrew.

By the time the first exiles returned home under Zerubbabel (538 BCE), few people spoke Hebrew regularly although it remained the language for prayer and reading the Scriptures. Aramaic, therefore, became the regular *lingua franca* of the region. Four hundred years later, it was still a common language for that part of the world where Jesus lived.

By this time the Romans ruled the Mediterranean world and beyond, but the international language was Greek. This was because of Alexander the Great's conquests three centuries earlier and the resultant spread of Greek culture across his empire. We associate Latin with the Romans and almost certainly they spoke a conversational type of Latin amongst themselves which, say the linguists, depended less on case and declension than

does the classical Latin with which many of us struggled at school.

Nevertheless, even Rome needed Greek to administer its dominions. It was the one language which everyone understood. This is why the New Testament is written in Greek, despite theories that early sources for some of the gospels were in Hebrew or Aramaic. Pilate wrote the inscription on the cross in Latin, Greek and Hebrew. He probably spoke Greek at the trial of Jesus.

We can assume, then, that Jesus and his compatriots spoke Aramaic publicly and a good deal of Hebrew amongst themselves. The assumption is that it was a simple, colloquial Hebrew, similar to that in which the Mishnah is written. They used Greek with foreigners, in so far as Jews were willing to talk to non-Jews at all. They doubtless had a better grasp of Latin than they would ever admit to the hated Roman officials and probably took much delight in pretending not to understand it. For all religious purposes they used a pure, classical Hebrew.

Linguistic Helps in Understanding the Bible

No translation, however good, can do justice to the original. Some understanding of both Hebrew and Greek will offer new insights into familiar passages and generally enhance our appreciation of the Bible. Before offering some specific examples, the following information is worth keeping in mind.

Hebrew words are mostly formed from three-letter roots, each carrying a basic idea. According to specific rules, one tri-literal root can be built up into many words with widely differing meanings yet all related to the root concept. Greek words, too, have their own fundamental definition but there is an interesting difference between the two languages. Hebrew roots express an essential, underlying cause whereas the corresponding Greek word tends to describe the effect of the cause. Look for this in some of the examples given overleaf.

Hebrew vocabulary is not particularly extensive and is poor in synonyms. Therefore, one word may cover a range of application which would utilise three or four words in a language such as Greek or English. By contrast, Greek has a wide vocabulary and is rich in synonyms. It also has an array of prepositions, prefixes and tenses which bring subtle distinctions to the meaning of a word and allow great precision of expression.

Greek inscription from a city gate at Thessalonica. Greek was the one language everyone understood.

One final point is worth noting. It was not hard in a polytheistic society for the New Testament writers to find Greek equivalents for Hebrew religious concepts. The only problem was that the Greek word often carried associations with the idolatrous system from which it originated. It might be adequate and it could absorb new connotations but it easily lost some subtle flavour of the monotheistic, Hebrew system which it represented. Here, then, are some examples of how a knowledge of Hebrew enriches our understanding of the Bible.

Four Problems Solved

1. To Go or Not to Go

When Balak sent messengers to Balaam asking him to curse Israel, God instructed, 'Do not go with them'.[1] More emissaries then came and tried to change Balaam's mind. Now God says, 'Arise and go with them', yet when Balaam does so, God is angry. Why? Is he being capricious or unfair? Jewish scholars solve the difficulty by pointing out that two words are used in the passage for 'with'; *it* and *im*. *It* denotes mere physical proximity. *Im* implies a togetherness of motive and intention.

God first told Balaam, 'Do not go *im* them'. He was not to associate in any way with their plans, neither by his presence nor his sympathies. On the second occasion, God said, 'Go *it* them'. He could accompany them, but must on no account support their cause. However, when Balaam set off we are told that he went '*im* the men from Moab'. Deep down he was willing to curse Israel if he got the chance. Perhaps he hoped God would change his mind. This is why God was angry.

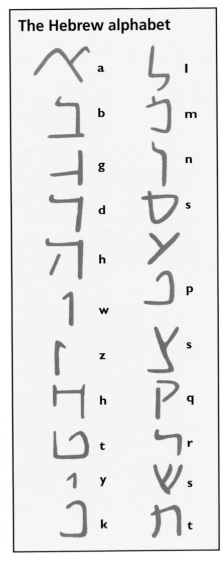

The Hebrew alphabet

a

b

g

d

h

w

z

h

t

y

k

l

m

n

s

p

s

q

r

s

t

The Greek alphabet

A	A	K	K
B	B	Λ	L
Γ	G	M	M
Δ	D	N	N
E	E	Ξ	
Y	F/Y	O	O
Z	Z	Γ	P
H	H	P	R
⊙	TH	Σ	S
I	I	T	T

2. Bless the Lord, O My soul!

It is easy to see how God can bless us but how can we bless him? God blesses us with many material favours as well as spiritual benefits. Being himself the source of all good, he needs none of these things from us. The answer lies in understanding the Hebrew for blessing. It is *berakhah*, from the root *b-r-kh* which carries the idea of bowing, bending the knee. The word for a knee, *berekh*, is from the same root.

If we follow this meaning through, we soon find the question reversed. It is now easy to see how we can bless God as, metaphorically, we bow reverentially before him but how can he bless us? God neither bows nor subjects himself to anyone and he will not give his glory to any other.

By contrast, in humbling himself to become a God of immanence as well as of transcendence, God voluntarily limits and conceals his glory, though he never denies it. His greatest act of concealment and limitation was, of course, the incarnation, when he 'reduced' himself to take on human form. That is his richest blessing for all humankind from which all other divine blessings spring.

It is also worth noting that in many cases, a word translated as 'blessed' sometimes comes from the Hebrew *asher*, meaning happy. The first word in Psalm 1 is an example. Rather than 'Blessed is the man', we should read, 'Happy is the man', as some translations do.

3. A Scapegoat for Azazel

During the Day of Atonement, Israel's sins were confessed over the head of a scapegoat. It was then sent into the desert for Azaze.[2] Who, or what, is Azazel? Some commentators see Azazel as a satyr or demon who had to be appeased. This seems silly in view of the prohibition in the next chapter against making offerings to satyrs.[3]

The Greek Septuagint translation of the Old Testament often throws light on difficult Hebrew words. It renders Azazel as a common noun meaning 'the one to be sent away'. A former Chief Rabbi, Dr Hertz, refers to a rare word, *azlazel*, which is a technical term for the removal of sin or dismissal. Linguistically an -l easily disappears. *Azazel*, contracted from *azlazel*, is the goat which is sent away or dismissed. It was not sent into the desert for some deity called *Azazel* but for an *Azlazel*, or removal of sin.

4. The Head of the Bed

Shortly before Jacob died, he made Joseph promise to bury him in Canaan with his forefathers. Different versions of the Scriptures then describe how he raised himself over the head of his bed, drew his feet into the bed or bowed himself upon the bed's head. The book of Hebrews says that he leaned upon his staff.[4] What actually happened?

The confusion comes from the fact that there are two Hebrew words whose consonants are identical but whose vowels differ. One is *mittah*, generally translated as bed. The other is *matteh*, which is a staff. Because the ancient Hebrew texts use consonants only, words like *mittah* and *matteh* were easily confused. It was only round about the sixth century CE that vowel signs were added to help clarify and preserve the meaning for later readers.

Almost certainly, Hebrew gives the correct rendering of this event. As Joseph and his father made their pact, Jacob bent over his staff in some kind of ritual acknowledgement of what was happening. More importantly, his staff had a specific implication. It was not a stick to give support but was part of the insignia of office that a clan chief carried.

When the tribes challenged the right of Moses and Aaron to lead the community, God told the head of each tribe to bring his staff to the Tabernacle. Overnight, Aaron's staff budded as a sign that he and Moses were God's choice for the task, even though they did not belong to the tribe of Reuben, Jacob's eldest son.[5]

Some translations use the term 'branch', probably feeling it is more appropriate in view of the miracle that one of the rods budded and produced fruit, all in one night. This is not a wrong translation but it appears to miss the significance of the fact that the *matteh* was the symbol of patriarchal status.

Four Theological Insights

1. Teach Us How to Pray

There are many words for prayer in both Greek and Hebrew. They reflect all aspects of this spiritual activity. The verb most often used in Hebrew is *hitpallel*, from the root *P-L-L* denoting, not request, but judgement. Most common in Greek is *proseuche*, a pouring out of supplication.

At first, the Hebrew link with judgement is puzzling and yet, on consideration, it offers insights into the fundamental concept of prayer of which elements such as supplication are but part. The Hebrew form of the verb to pray is reflexive. We deduce, therefore, that prayer is an act of self-judgement.

This means that when we pray we must assess our own spiritual state so that we pray

The Jewish scriptures would have been written on scrolls like this.

with a right attitude towards God and other people. We must ask ourselves what certain prayer commitments will entail and if we will be able to cope if we get involved. Can we be trusted with the answer? Will we give God the glory or overestimate the worth of our own contribution?

We must also judge the content of our prayers in the light of God's laws and character. Seen in that perspective, there are some things we cannot ask for. Mere 'shopping lists' and prayers which challenge God or distort Scripture are not acceptable. Our judgement is faulty. Will we let God, the only infallible judge

of a situation, make the final decision? 'Thy will be done' can be a get out clause, a sop to lack of faith. We can only say it properly in a spirit of renunciation as we submit to God's omniscient ways. In this sense, all that we 'ask in his name', he does.[6]

2. Peace, Perfect Peace

Countless Christians know the word *shalom*, peace; but what is peace? Serenity? Contentment? Quietude? The Greek *eirene* means concord and unity. However, these things are the outcome rather than the essence of peace, as the Hebrew root SH-L-M implies. It means completeness and wholeness.

When people or nations have opposing ideals and share no common cause, relationships are fragmented and broken. When a person grapples with deep, unresolved conflicts, there is no inner wholeness. Unity of purpose, agreement of principle, differences reconciled and common direction bring wholeness to relationships and to the inner being. This is peace. It is not dependent on everything being in order or to one's liking. It functions in spite of adversity and, from its own unimpaired base of security, can confront and change circumstances.

3. At-one-ment

Preachers sometimes say, 'Atonement means at-one-ment'. What they should say is, 'Atonement achieves at-one-ment'. The Hebrew is *kippur* from the root, *K-P-R*, which means a covering. The Greek *katallage* means reconciliation. In short, when sin is covered, reconciliation is effected.

The Day of Atonement rituals described in Leviticus 16 endorse this interpretation. Amongst them are confession of sin and its transference to a sacrificial animal by laying hands on the victim's head. The blood from the sacrifice is sprinkled on a variety of objects and people in order to atone for sin and uncleanness. It 'covers' the sin, thereby hiding it from the sight of a holy God.

No one symbol can express the complete truth, so that the rites of the scapegoat add a further dimension. Here, sin is symbolically transferred to a live animal which then carries it away into a desert place. The scapegoat typifies the permanent removal of sin. Of course,

the imagery of covering and removal point to the New Testament reality. The blood of Jesus both covers and removes our sin and thereby reconciles us to God.

4. A Weight of Glory

'Glory' in the Bible is an experience rather than a theoretical concept. It is described in words like brightness and resplendence but that is only part of the story. Biblical glory is associated with the God of Israel rather than other deities, so we look to the Hebrew for its authentic meaning. *Doxa*, in Greek primarily signifies an opinion or estimate and hence, the honour resulting from a good opinion. The Hebrew *Kavod* is from the root *K-V-D* denoting heaviness; not something one immediately associates with glory.

The connection becomes clear as we examine biblical experiences of glory. Whenever God reveals himself, be it to Moses,[7] Daniel,[8] Isaiah,[9] Ezekiel,[10] at the Transfiguration,[11] to Paul at his conversion,[12] or to disclose the revelation to John at Patmos,[13] the magnificent splendour of the vision is overwhelming. The recipients fall flat on their faces or become ill or as dead men. It weighs them down like a burden too heavy to handle.

In talking of 'an eternal weight of glory', Paul may have written in Greek but he was surely thinking in Hebrew.[14] When life gets hard for a Christian, it helps to realise that the loads we carry are a refining process. If accepted with the right attitude, they will help to eliminate all the things like pride, resentment and self-will which cannot stand before the glory of the Holy God. When we meet him face to face, we shall be fully perfected. That process begins now.

John the Baptist appeared in the wilderness of Judaea.

Fresh Light in Familiar Places

1. The Wilderness Shall Blossom
The Israelites were nomads for forty years in the wilderness. John the Baptist appeared preaching in the wilderness of Judaea. The Greek word *eremos* describes a deserted, desolate place. The Hebrew *midbar*, though sometimes translated desert or wilderness, is by no means a barren waste. It is rather an area with such limited rainfall that it cannot support regular crops. Hence, it is not permanently settled and 'not sown'. It only needs a regular water supply to be intensely fertile.

The *midbar* was, and is, communal grazing ground. In summer it provides sparse fare but shepherds know where to lead their flocks to get the most from the thorns and scrub that survive the parching sun. In winter, after a few showers, the earth blossoms and the flocks feast.

2. Puns on Places
The Old Testament is full of puns and allusions which are lost in translation. For instance, people's names are usually significant, as with Jacob's twelve sons.[15] Micah links eleven towns with God's judgements as follows.[16] We do our best but it is not easy to make the puns entirely clear in any other language than Hebrew.

'Tell it not in Gath' was a proverb coined by David at Saul's death. In Hebrew, Gath also sounds similar to the word *tagidu*, tell. Beth Le'aphrah pairs with the word for dust, *aphar*. Shaphir can describe something which is pleasant or fine but the context links it with sounding the *shophar* or ram's horn. Zaanan is associated with *yotzeah*, she has gone out. Beth Etzel is connected to *atzal*, to withhold, in the sense that its standing place would be withheld or removed from its site.

Maroth joins with *mar*, meaning bitterness. Lachish stands alongside *rechesh*, a chariot steed. Trading in war horses instead of trusting God may be the sin referred to here. Moresheth-Gath suggests the word *meorashah* for the betrothed and the bride dowry to be paid. Beth Achzib is a play on *achzab*, deception. Mareshah has the same root as *yoresh* and the idea of a conqueror plundering for booty. David fled to Adullam from Saul. Israel will again need such a refuge when judgement strikes.

3. David and Goliath

Can anyone say anything new about this beloved story?[17] Then how about this interpretation offered by a rabbi? Goliath wore armour. His helmet, as archaeological finds show, would fully protect the bridge of his nose and his brow. How, then, could the stone sink into his forehead without being deflected? Even had he carelessly removed his helmet, a blow on the temple should have sent him reeling backwards rather than onto his face.

The answer lies in the Hebrew word for forehead, *metzach*. This could easily be confused with a related word, *mitzchah*, meaning greaves, which were pieces of leg armour like cricket pads. Both words share the root M-TZ-CH.

Imagine that David aimed his stone, not at the well protected *metzach*, forehead, but at the *mitzchah*, one of the greaves. The stone hit the upper leg and sank into the space which allowed the knee to bend. The giant lunged at David. The stone wedged, unexpectedly and painfully against his shin. It threw him off balance and he fell forward. He was not hurt but his unwieldy armour immobilised him long enough for David to grab Goliath's own sword and kill him.

If you prefer the familiar version, at least enjoy some fun with this one. It could, just, be the right one. Be aware that different, perhaps more accurate understandings, can be culled from the Hebrew original.

That Which Goes Forth

The first five books of the Bible are called the *Torah* and the word is used countless times in the Hebrew Scriptures. Invariably translated as Law, a more accurate term is instruction. It is quite correct that the Torah does contain religious, legal material, but it also provides a framework of narrative and commentary from which the laws spring and in which they function.

The root, *Y-R-H*, from which *Torah* comes, carries the idea of going forth or being sent out. It gives rise to words like an arrow, which goes forth from the bow; an archer, one who releases the arrow; and to shoot. A teacher, someone who gives out information, comes from the same root. Thus, *Torah* is a body of instruction which is given out.

The root meaning is not concerned with where or how what is given out will end up. Other words are used to describe the target for the arrow or the pupil who receives and learns what is taught. The root turns us back to sources rather than ahead to targets. This surely says something about the traditional Jewish and Christian belief that the Torah comes from God by an act of revelation. Its validity is determined by its source, not its recipients, reception or results.

In Conclusion

Few people have the privilege of knowing Hebrew or Greek. Most of us depend upon translations for reading the Bible. For anyone who has found this chapter interesting, it is worth buying a good concordance and a study Bible with notes and a cross-reference system. They are not substitutes for linguistic facility

THE LANGUAGE JESUS SPOKE 61

but they are a great help in many areas.

How amazing that, despite variations or shortcomings in a translation, the words of the Bible still speak to our hearts, be it in rebuke, challenge, comfort or guidance! Is not this the most telling proof we can offer for the doctrine of the inspiration of the Scriptures? Above all, does it not encourage us to study our Bible with greater diligence and trust in its relevance for all situations?

Bible references

1 Numbers 22:12–22
2 Leviticus 16:7–10, 20–22
3 Leviticus 17:7
4 Genesis 47:31;
   Hebrews 11:21
5 Numbers 17
6 John 14:14
7 Exodus 3:6; 20:19;
   33:18–33
8 Isaiah 6:1–17
9 Ezekiel 1:28; 3:12–15
10 Daniel 8:17, 18, 27;
    Daniel 10:7–11, 15–19
11 Matthew 17:1–8
12 Acts 9:1–9
13 Revelation 1:12–17
14 2 Corinthians 4:17
15 Genesis 29:31—30:24;
    35:16–20
16 Micah 1:10–16
17 1 Samuel 17

CHAPTER SIX

The Countryside Jesus Crossed

The setting of the Bible is rural, for even most of the so-called cities were more like small towns compared with today. Jesus and his disciples followed an itinerant lifestyle and were well travelled in their immediate surroundings. Almost certainly they walked wherever they went. Their journeys were facilitated by a good network of paved roads which the Romans always engineered in the places they governed.

A physical map of the Holy Land clearly shows four strips of terrain running parallel with the Mediterranean coast. Our present concern is mostly with the area south of modern Lebanon.

The Coastal Plain

The coastal plain is no more than ten miles wide. It has a hot, humid climate but it is fertile and populous inland from the sand dunes. In the time of the kingdoms of Israel and Judah, the Philistines occupied the south while some Jewish tribes lived further north. Much of it, however, was a Gentile enclave, for Israel was not really a maritime nation.

The area between Tel Aviv and Haifa is the Plain of Sharon. Until fairly recent times, the coastal sand dunes encroached well inland. Under the State of Israel, much land has been reclaimed by planting shrubs to stabilise the sand. Here the rose of Sharon grows.[1] It seems that it was not actually a rose but a bulb plant, as the Hebrew indicates. It is a richly scented narcissus type of flower which grows wild among the dunes.

An important trade route followed the coast. Armies, too, constantly passed that way as the balance of power forever see-sawed between Egypt and the lands to the north and east. Main ports were Jaffa (near Tel Aviv), visited by Jonah and Peter; Caesarea thirty miles up the coast and connected with Peter, Cornelius and Paul as well as being the home of the Roman governors of Palestine; and Ptolemais (modern Acre north of Haifa) also associated with Paul. Apart from a visit to the Tyre and Sidon area in Lebanon, Jesus never frequented the coast, as far as we know.[2]

The Mountain Strip

Parallel with the coastal plain, a mountain chain extends north from the Negev desert to meet Mount Carmel. It then yields to the plains of Zebulon and Jezreel which cut

rael:
owing
e four strips
terrain

Tyre

PLAIN OF PHOENICIA

Dan

Mt. Hermon
(9,232ft / 2,184m)

Lake Huleh

SYRIAN DESERT

ARAM

GREAT SEA
(MEDITERRANEAN SEA)

Mt. Carmel
(1,732ft / 528m)

Tiberias

SEA OF CHINNERETH
(SEA OF GALILEE)

PLAIN OF SHARON

VALLEY OF JEZREEL

Mt. Tabor
(1,929ft / 588m)

Yarmuk

GILEAD

Mt. Gilboa
(1,630ft / 497m)

Jordan

Mt. Ebal
(3,083ft / 940m)

Samaria

Mt. Gerizim
(2,889ft / 881m)

Jabbok

HILLS OF EPHRAIM

ISRAEL

AMMON

Joppa

THE ARABAH

Bethel

Jericho

PLAIN OF PHILISTIA

Mt. of Olives
(2,723ft / 830m)

kelon

Jerusalem

SHEPHELAH

JUDAH

Mt. Nebo
(2,630ft / 802m)

Gaza

HILLS OF JUDEA

WILDERNESS OF JUDEA

Hebron

SALT SEA (DEAD SEA)

OASTAL
TRIP

Arnon

MOAB

Beersheba

0   25   50 km

MOUNTAIN
AND HILLS

0   10   20   30 miles

metres   feet
1,000   3,281
500   1,640
200   656
0   0
below sea   below sea
level   level

THE NEGEB

Zered

THE ARABAH

RIFT VALLEY   HIGH PLATEAU

EDOM

inwards from the Bay of Haifa. The mountains return in northern Galilee, rising to the peak of Hermon and on into Lebanon. The climate is drier on the high ground and the strong, summer heat is tempered by the altitude. In winter the mountains are very cold.

The plains of Zebulon and Jezreel were fertile but swampy. The fact that they flooded in winter contributed to Sisera's defeat. Having said this, kings generally went to war during the summer when it was dry. The record seems to imply that there was an unseasonal storm. The river Kishon overflowed its banks, as it always used to do before the Israelis drained the malarial swamps and cultivated the land thus reclaimed. Sisera's chariots were caught in the deluge and were bogged down in the mud. He had to flee on foot. Did the early rains come a lot sooner than he expected?[3]

Today the plains are well drained and exceptionally fertile. By contrast, the rocky mountains are impossible to farm, except where a terracing system brings the lower slopes under cultivation. Only the narrow wadis (valleys) between them are easy to cultivate.

Here Jesus was at home. Nazareth lies at the edge of the plains in the foothills of Upper Galilee. Nearby are Cana where he performed his first miracle and Nain where he raised the widow's son to life. Many earlier events also occurred around this area. Deborah judged at Mount Tabor, Gideon defeated the Midianites and Saul and Jonathan died in battle at Mount Gilboa. Solomon equipped a strategic fortress at Megiddo, Elijah visited Mount Carmel and Ahab had a palace in Jezreel.

On one occasion Jesus visited Caesarea Philippi at the headwaters of the Jordan. There Peter declared belief in his Messiahship.

Mount Tabor, where Deborah judged.

Shortly after, the Transfiguration took place. Most scholars hold that it happened on the nearby slopes of Mount Hermon rather than at the traditional site of Mount Tabor further south. The element of doubt is due to uncertainty as to whether Jesus himself went apart from the crowds or whether it was the mountain which stood apart.

Archaeology shows that there was human activity on Tabor which might have made it difficult to find a private place. Nor is Tabor a very high mountain. It only appears so because it stands alone, rising from the plain like a huge dome. By contrast, Hermon is high and more isolated. Mark's version also says that Jesus' clothes were white like snow. Was the simile prompted by the snow that lies in crevices on the top of Hermon all year round? Snow never even falls on Tabor.[4]

Southwards stretched the direct route from Galilee to Judaea through hilly Samaria. Few Jews used it. Between Jews and Samaritans lay too much history of hatred and they preferred to go down the rift valley towards Jericho and then cut west into the hills up to Jerusalem. Jesus only went that way in order to minister to the woman at the well at Sychar.[5]

The well was on land which Jacob bought from Shechem. Five hundred years later, Joseph's descendants still had the title deeds. They buried him there when they entered Canaan and not in Hebron with his fore-fathers.[6] Tourists can still visit the well on the outskirts of Nablus and drink its water and see the traditional site of Joseph's tomb near by.

The Rift Valley

Forty miles inland is the third strip, a deep rift valley about five miles wide along most of its length. The Jordan starts at Mount Hermon at the top of the rift. It descends into Lake

The snow-capped peaks of Mount Hermon, where scholars believe the Transfiguration occurred.

Galilee, six hundred and fifty feet below sea level. It then emerges to wind seventy miles further into the Dead Sea, over a thousand feet below sea level. The dry valley continues to the Gulf of Aqaba and on into Africa. At times the rift widens into cultivated ground, but close to the river its tangled undergrowth still gives refuge to wild animals as it did in Bible days.

Below sea level the climate is sub-tropical, which makes for hot, enervating summers and pleasant winters. For this reason Herod Antipas, who killed John the Baptist, built Tiberias on Lake Galilee as a winter resort. Energy dwindles in the intense summer heat of the Galilee basin when the hills on either side are parched and brown. Everyone welcomes the mild winters when, for a few brief weeks, the rains transform the landscape with fresh greens and vivid flowers.

As one plant species withers, another blooms. At one point, delicate crane's bill florets dye the ground pink. Later in the season, yellow mustard flowers cover the fields. These are different from the much rarer mustard tree, alluded to by Jesus. On this tall, more sturdy plant, the birds can comfortably perch. It is not a tree but it does have a thick stem and short branches and can grow over six feet tall.[7] Jesus was probably referring to the wild, scarlet anemones when he said, 'Consider the lilies of the field'.[8]

Because much of his ministry took place beside the lake in fishing towns such as Capernaum and Bethsaida, Jesus was also familiar with the sudden storms which funnelled through the narrow rift valley and raised great waves on the lake's surface. They start when hot air from the land meets the cooler air from the water to create eddying currents of wind. Though short lived, the squalls are dangerous to small boats such as the disciples owned.[9]

In the late 1980s, during a time of drought, the level of the lake fell to a very low state and revealed the skeleton of a boat from around that period. It was salvaged and preserved and is now on view to show us the kind of craft which the disciples probably used.

Transjordan and Beyond

The fourth strip of land is a high plateau east of the Jordan valley which disappears into the Arabian desert. The weather is hot and dry.

Tiberias stands on the shores of Lake Galilee.

Carefully preserved remains of the skeleton of a Galilee boat from around the time of Jesus.

Most Gospel stories occurred down in the rift valley or in the Judaean and Galilean highlands but many Old Testament events are associated with the coastal plain and the countries beyond Jordan.

The patriarchs originated in Chaldea. Jacob lived with Laban in Haran. The end of the forty years in the wilderness is set in Edom, Moab, Ammon and Bashan—countries immediately east of the river Jordan. Two-and-a-half tribes chose to inherit the good grazing land on the Transjordan plateau. Daniel, Ezekiel, Ezra, Nehemiah and Esther all describe events in Babylonia and Assyria, the countries of the captivity to the east.

Cycle of the Year

The weather in Bible lands is very different from that of the western world and it helps our Bible understanding to know its patterns. After seven months of summer drought the ground is rock hard. By October a little light rain is needed to soften the earth enough to start the ploughing which, in Bible times, was impossible before the rain came with the simple tools available. It is important that the early rains are light. Heavy rain merely sweeps away the top soil.

Ploughing and sowing are completed by mid-December before the rains intensify. Then winter sets in, a season of mild sunshine interspersed with storm and cold. Wild flowers bloom, the grass grows and trees put out early blossom. Winter cedes to spring in February. The sun strengthens and the rains lessen until, by the end of April, they have almost ceased.

By this time the grain is turning gold ready for reaping. Barley ripens first, followed later by the wheat. The harvest is in by mid-June and then the threshing and winnowing, so often referred to in the Bible, are finished at leisure. Summer is the time for figs, pomegranates, dates, grapes, olives, melons, onions, cucumbers, leeks and many non-biblical species too.

It is amazing how crops survived the dry heat of July and August before modern systems of artificial irrigation were introduced. Some flourished in naturally irrigated spots near a spring. Others were watered by hand from a local well. Yet others, particularly near the coast, drew in moisture from mists and dews. But by September the summer crops are gathered in, the cycle of the year draws to its close and the whole process is ready to start afresh.

Telling the seasons

So many Bible stories happened when and how they did because of seasonal, climatic factors. Understanding the seasons helps us to work these things out. It may not always greatly contribute to our spiritual blessing but, if nothing else, it is intellectually satisfying, as the following examples show.

In order to bring back fresh summer fruits, the twelve spies must have explored Canaan during July and August.[10] Gideon was threshing wheat when God called him to rescue Israel from Midian. As wheat is reaped in late spring, it had to be around June.[11] Naomi and Ruth came to Bethlehem at the beginning of barley harvest. Barley ripens before wheat s[o] the story took place from April onwards.[12]

Elijah called Elisha as he was ploughing with twelve yoke of oxen, one day in Novembe[r] or early December.[13] Elisha did not necessaril[y] own the twenty-four oxen nor was he handling them alone. Peasant farmers worked together much as the old Shetland crofters used to d[o] when a row of women, each with a spade, worked as a team to dig each person's field i[n] turn.

Disaster hit Job's servants at the same tim[e] of year, when they were also ploughing.[14] Jesus fed the five thousand in a place where ther[e] was much green grass. Down by Lake Galile[e] this could only be in winter during the rainy season, most likely in January.[15] The disciples plucked ripe corn one Sabbath in May, jus[t] prior to the reaping.[16]

Local Features and Phenomena

As Bible characters pass before our eyes, everywhere the features and phenomena of the countryside which bred them come to life in their stories and writings. We illustrate with the instances below.

Heatwave and Night Mists

When the heavens are like brass and the earth as iron, the heat is exceptionally vicious.[17] There is either drought or a *sharav*; a ho[t] desert wind which blows in spring and autumn. Then the dust in the atmosphere gives the sky a yellowish hue and the air shimmers in a haze of heat which persists relentlessly through the night. In times of drought, all vegetation withers and the ground becomes rock hard so that no primitive plough or spade

The northern shore of Lake Galilee in spring, when there is still plenty of green grass.

can dent it. Man and beast long for a cool breeze and moisture. It is a telling picture of God's judgement.

Even without a heatwave, there is never any rain in summer. Natural vegetation is sustained by dews and mists. Did Jesus ever rise in the summer dawn to climb the hills above Nazareth? Did he ever look across to Mount Carmel and see the plain below covered with low lying, white cloud from which the surrounding mountains emerge like islands? This is the night mist which forms in the summer because the Carmel range is so close to the sea. As soon as the sun rises, it disappears.

Hosea saw the same phenomenon and compared it to Israel's short-lived repentance.[18] The mist covers stones and vegetation during the night like rain. Rocks under trees are wet and fat globules of water form on windows and metal railings. It keeps the scrub growth

of Mount Carmel green all through the dry season when inland hills are bare and brown. There is drought indeed when the mist fails and Carmel withers, as the prophets knew.[19]

Flash Floods[20]

One day Israel, Judah and Edom set out to fight against Moab. Caught out with no water for their troops and animals, they consulted Elisha. He assured them that although they would not see wind or rain, the dry stream bed would be filled with water. Next day it happened as he had foretold. The Moabites also saw the water. Reflecting the rising sun, it looked like blood and deceived them into thinking that the kings had fought amongst themselves.

Apparently an early fall of heavy rain in the hills above sent sudden torrents of water cascading down the dry, stony valley. Flash floods come without warning. They wash away topsoil, displace boulders and even sweep away shepherds with their flocks and vehicles on the roads. Once the worst is over, the pools and streams that remain reflect light and colour, as in this story.

In Israel, a few people are killed in flash floods almost every year when the early rains begin. In this story, it all surely happened in the late summer but well before the early rains were due; hence the element of miracle and surprise. Was the Psalmist thinking of the strength of a flash flood which carries everything with it when he sang, 'Lord, bring all our captives back again like torrents in the Negev'?[21]

Springs, Wells, Cisterns and Aqueducts
In limestone country, there are natural, underground reservoirs which feed springs and wells. In a hidden valley on Mount Carmel, a spring trickles from a cleft rock, summer and winter alike. Immediately below flourishes a small orchard of pomegranate trees. The Romans took water from springs in the foothills of Carmel by aqueduct to Caesarea down the coast. Tourists still see its arches rising from the sand dunes.

In the territory of Samaria, another valley stays green all summer because it is irrigated from an ever flowing source. Beside the road through the valley is a small spring which a local villager uses as a fridge in summer. He keeps a supply of bottled drinks cool under the cascading water. Here is the site of Tirzah. Tirzah was Israel's old capital before Omri bought a field from Shemer and built a new capital which he called Shomron or Samaria.[22]

There are wells all over the country, many

very ancient, for no settlement could survive without them in bygone times. Wells are simply holes in the ground surrounded by a low wall covered with a stone slab.

To water Rachel's sheep, Jacob moved a stone which normally took the combined power of a number of men.[23] At the traditional site of Elijah's sacrifice on Carmel is a well which, they say, never runs dry. After three years' drought, it was probably the only water source for miles around which Elijah could have used to soak his sacrifice.[24]

Cisterns are made from plastered stones or hewn from bedrock. Country people used the village well. In the towns, most houses had a

Underground water cistern at Hazor.

Remains of the Roman aqueduct built to bring a constant water supply to the port and administrative centre of Caesarea Maritima.

cistern underneath where water accumulated for use in the summer. The Old City of Jerusalem is honeycombed with them, and some are huge. Jeremiah was thrown into a dry cistern—it must have been summer—but he still sank deeply into the mud.[25] In Second Temple days, they also brought water to Jerusalem by aqueduct from catchment pools some miles away from the city.

Plastered cisterns needed regular upkeep to stay waterproof, otherwise the precious water soon leaked away. This is what Jeremiah had in mind when he spoke of broken cisterns.[26] Tourists in the Negev can see remains of the ancient Nabatean cisterns which they built to preserve water for the dry summers.

Litany of Curse and Blessing

When Israel entered Canaan, six tribes gathered on Mount Ebal and six on Mount Gerizim opposite, to recite a litany of blessings and cursings.[27] A preacher once questioned the tale, suggesting that two groups of people on two mountains would not hear each other well enough to perform an antiphonal ceremony. He had never visited the spot.

There is a quarry on the lower slopes of Ebal. If you stand opposite on Gerizim, the sound of a pickaxe on stone rings across the valley like a tenor bell. You can almost distinguish the words of a solitary workman calling to his mate, such are the acoustics of the place. No wonder that Gideon's son chose to stand on the lower slopes of Gerizim to shout his protest to the elders in the city of Shechem below, before he fled for safety.[28]

Modern Nablus now fills the valley between Gerizim and Ebal and travellers going north or

The traditional site of Jacob's well, Sychar.

south still traverse this mountain pass. At its southern end is Sychar and the sites of Jacob's well and Joseph's tomb.

When Jesus journeyed through Samaria, did he recall how Joshua built an altar on Mount Ebal to celebrate Israel's entry into the promised land?[29] In 1980 an Israeli archaeologist unearthed a large altar of unhewn stones, half a mile from the summit of Ebal and of the Joshua period. Significantly, he found only the bones of ritually clean animals and no heathen figurines. The altar is almost identical to that of the Second Temple described in the Mishnah and, despite a century of searching, nothing else has been discovered. Such facts suggest that this could be the very altar raised by Joshua.

High Places

As Jesus walked through Samaria, how conscious was he of being near to the capital of the northern kingdom of Israel and the close association of its tribes with Canaanite cults and high places? A high place was a grove of sacred trees on some hill top where an altar and cultic objects stood and where idolatrous, and often obscene, rites were enacted.

For the most part in Samaria today, the hills are bare and stony. Yet in places, tree clad bluffs unexpectedly arise from the barrenness. Most obvious is Mount Ebal itself. Its empty rocky ridge clearly ends in a peak. There, surrounding the summit, is a thick, green cap of trees. We do not know whether these features are of ancient or more recent origin but we have noticed them repeatedly in travelling through that area.

Are they the relics of ancient high places? Who can tell, but in some instances it may be so. It would certainly account for Joshua raising his altar at a distance from the peak of Ebal and lower. Arab villagers also point out sacred trees and groves and who knows what history lies behind them? One or two Israeli *kibbutzim* are built on land which traditionally is said to cover one of the high places. If such sights and traditions exist today, what might Jesus have seen as he traversed Samaria, so much nearer to those idolatrous times?

Mount Gerizim and Mount Ebal dominate the modern city of Nablus, biblical Sychar.

Bible references

1	Song of Songs 2:1	10	Numbers 13:21–25
2	Mark 7:24	11	Judges 6:11–13
3	Judges 5:20, 21	12	Ruth 1:22
4	Mark 9:2,3	13	1 Kings 19:19
5	John 4:5	14	Job 1:14
6	Genesis 33:18,19	15	Mark 6:39; John 6:10
	Joshua 24:32	16	Matthew 12:1
7	Mark 4:31, 32	17	Deuteronomy 28:23, 24
8	Matthew 6:28 RSV	18	Hosea 13:3
9	Mark 4:35–41	19	Amos 1:2; Nahum 1:4
		20	2 Kings 3
		21	Psalm 126:4

22	1 Kings 16:23, 24
23	Genesis 29:1–10
24	1 Kings 18:34, 35
25	Jeremiah 38:6
26	Jeremiah 2:13
27	Deuteronomy 27
	Joshua 8:32–35
28	Judges 9:7
29	Joshua 8:30, 31
	Judges 9:7

CHAPTER SEVEN

Agricultural Methods Jesus Observed

If you wish to understand the agricultural ways of Bible days, visit any isolated Middle Eastern Arab village. There you can still see the old style of doing things and the same implements being used which the Bible writers constantly refer to as they tell their stories and illustrate their message.

Ploughing and Sowing

Once the early rains have softened the soil, ploughing begins, quickly followed by sowing. The farmer yokes his plough to either one or two animals. The task is easier with a double yoke but for the comfort of the animals they

A simple horse- or ox-drawn plough.

A donkey-drawn plough near Bethlehem.

must be the same size. If a donkey is put with an ox or, worse still, a camel, the yoke lies awkwardly across their necks and chafes them both.

This is why the Torah forbids using different species together and why Paul told Christians not to yoke themselves in marriage with unbelievers.[1] An easy yoke fits comfortably and allows the beasts to work well. Jesus said that when his followers walk and work, yoked together with him, the discipline involved is not onerous.[2]

Unlike our own old-fashioned ploughs which, where they still exist, have two handles, the Bible lands' plough has only one. Jesus accurately talks of putting a hand, not hands, to the plough.[3] The other hand is left free to hold the goad.

The goad is a long pole with a sharp point at one end used to control an unbroken or difficult beast. Each time it kicks out, the ploughman ensures that its foot comes up against the point. It soon learns docility. The other end of the goad is shaped for scraping mud off the ploughshare and removing stones wedged in an animal's hoof. Paul, like a headstrong ox, kicked against the pricks of the truth that God was trying to show him.[4]

Ripening and Reaping

After ploughing, farmers sowed the seed by hand and Jesus noted how it fell in different places and flourished or withered accordingly.[5] He then compared the kingdom of heaven to a field where darnel grew amongst the wheat.[6]

Back-breaking work preparing the soil with a mattock

Darnel is indistinguishable from wheat until both are ripe. Then, the heavier wheat heads bend while the lighter darnel remains upright. Just before harvest, workers go through the fields picking it out. It is poisonous and can make people very ill if any is left and gets ground into the flour.

The months between Passover and Pentecost, April to June, are the harvest season. Appropriate grain ceremonies took place in the Temple at these times which we describe in a later chapter on the festivals. Barley ripens first while the wheat follows a few weeks later. This is why, in the story of the plagues, the hail destroyed the flax and barley but not the wheat and spelt which were less advanced.[7] Spelt was a kind of wild wheat.

In fact, an April storm at the beginning of the harvest is quite common, although one of such severity, which completely destroyed the early crops, was more unusual. A storm in May is almost unheard of. This makes the storm which God sent at wheat harvest, when the people asked Samuel for a king, to be a very salutary event.[8]

A sickle is a smaller implement than a scythe and it is more convenient for certain tasks. The word sickle or scythe is always used in the Bible in connection with reaping. It may be a simple command not to put your sickle into your neighbour's field to steal his crops. Sometimes it is a metaphor for reaping the harvest of souls at the end of the world.[9] Either way, farmers reaped the harvest by hand in this primitive way. They then stacked the produce at the threshing floor, ready for the next stage.

A threshing sledge.

Threshing and Winnowing

The threshing floor is a flat, rock surface on high, open ground which catches the summer breeze. There the farmer piles his crop and sets his oxen walking over it until the grain falls from the stalks. 'You shall not muzzle the ox,' states the Torah, 'when he treads the corn'. Paul uses this statement to back up his dictum that church leaders deserve proper support.[10]

When we read about Gideon threshing wheat in the wine press to hide it from the Midianites, it shows how completely subjugated and fearful his people were. Even a big wine press would make a very awkward threshing floor with no room to use the animals and proper equipment.[11]

The oxen then drag a wooden board, studded with metal, over the threshing floor to break up the long stalks and further separate the grain from them. This is the 'threshing sledge with teeth' to which Isaiah likened Israel's ultimate triumph over her persecutors.[12] David was at the threshing floor of Araunah the Jebusite when the plague in Israel ceased. He purchased it for the site of the Temple and bought the yokes and threshing sledges as wood for his sacrifice.[13]

A threshing roller is a rectangular wooden frame within which are rows of small wheels. It is surmounted by a seat where someone sits to give weight as its wheels cut up the straw. This contraption is mentioned with the sledge in an informative passage about ploughing, sowing and threshing.[14] In Latin it was called a *tribulum*, from which the word tribulation comes.

For winnowing, a good breeze is needed. A winnowing fork is a long handled tool with an array of wooden prongs fanning out at one end. With it the farmer expertly tosses the grain and broken straw into the air. In the process, the seed falls through the prongs while the straw stays on the fan to be set down elsewhere and the wind carries the insubstantial chaff away. In the verse about the mote and beam in someone's eye, the mote is probably a bit of chaff rather than a speck of dirt.[15]

Winnowing is a common figure of speech in the Bible where the good are compared to the grain and the wicked to the chaff which blows away.[16] John the Baptist said that the Messiah would come with his winnowing fan to gather

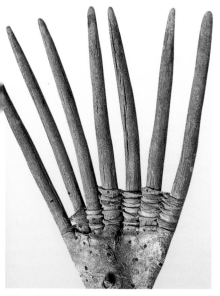

A fan-shaped winnowing fork

A winnowing fork.

the wheat into his barn and to burn up the chaff. In other words, the day will come when God will separate the useless from the profitable in the spiritual harvest of souls at the end of the age.[17]

Once the grain is stored, the oxen thresh the broken stalks of straw again. The longer the process, the finer they become. Crushed straw with barley is still animal fodder today, as it was in Solomon's time.[18] Hay is only used in countries with enough agricultural land and rain to grow large meadows of grass. A local saying went, 'No oxen, no cattle feed; stout ox, rich crop'.[19]

People also mixed crushed straw with clay to make the sun dried bricks which were used

in this part of the world. When Pharaoh refused to give the Israelites straw for the bricks they had to make, it was not just a case of scattering through Egypt to gather stubble left in the fields from the previous harvest. They then had to thresh it to the required grade before they could use it.[20]

Selling and Buying

Not everyone owned land and grew crops. If Joseph was a carpenter, he must have taught Jesus how to make yokes, plough frames, threshing sleds, winnowing fans and many other items. Other things, such as grain, the family would have to purchase in the market. As shopping was the father's job, we can imagine Joseph taking his sons with him to teach them how to make a good buy.

The grain merchant sits in the open, surrounded by heaps of barley and wheat which are roughly graded for quality. The buyer, always non-committal however interested in the wares he may be, looks around and decides which grain he wants. In the haggling that follows, the merchant quotes an exorbitant price. The buyer immediately offers a ridiculously low price. They finally settle on a mid-way sum which satisfies both.

The merchant then scoops the grain with his hands into a deep, round, wooden measure. Every so often the buyer picks it up and shakes the grain down. As the measure fills he presses the grain more compactly with his hands. Gradually it rises to a firm cone. When it seems no more can be added, he carefully sticks a finger into the peak, makes a tiny hollow and adds a few more grains until they run down the sides. This is a good measure, shaken, pressed down and running over. If this were not done, the measure might be about eleven pounds lighter. Jesus used the picture to show that the more generous our attitude to others, the more fully will we receive back.[21]

Preparing and Baking

The grain is bought in a very dirty state, full of pebbles, straw and dirt. Here starts the housewife's work. Seated on the ground, she puts some grain into a large sieve and shakes it sharply to bring big pieces of rubbish to the surface. These she removes. She then flicks the sieve around in a very precise motion while continuously blowing across it. Chaff, straw and dust are blown away. Tiny pieces of debris fall through the mesh. Pebbles are jerked to

A grain sieve.

one side and the good grain gathers in a heap in the centre of the sieve. Finally, she sorts through the grain by hand to ensure there is no darnel amongst it.

To sieve or sift a person implies a screening and proving process by way of hardship and temptation. Amos said that Israel was to be sifted among the nations like wheat before being eventually restored to its own land as a nation in a state of repentance and belief.[22] Even after two millennia in the diaspora, the Jewish people have survived. Now restored to nationhood, the prophecy is reaching the closing stages of its fulfilment.

Jesus told Peter that Satan wanted to sift him like wheat. The trials that followed showed Peter his weakness but failed to destroy him as Satan intended. Rather, they opened up his true potential. The good seed remained when the chaff and grit had been dispersed.[23]

Every home had its own millstones where flour was freshly ground each day for the family bread. So common were they that the archaeologists find them in every dig they

grain into the centre cavity and the stones, revolving against each other, ground it into flour.

Making the flour was always women's work. Male captives were given this task to demean them; as with Samson.[24] To take someone's millstone, even as a temporary pledge, was to deprive them of their basic, daily food. The Torah forbade it.[25] The daily sound of millstones at work indicated peace and prosperity.[26]

Many supermarkets sell pitta bread. It is like the bread of Bible days which was baked in a brick oven, probably a communal one used by all the village. Another kind of bread is made from a paste of flour and water but it is cooked differently. The housewife heats a metal dome, of about eighteen inches diameter, over a charcoal fire. She pours some of the mix over it which runs down the metal, cooking as it goes. Almost immediately she flips it over like a pancake and in seconds it is done. It is very tasty if eaten at once but it soon goes hard and stale.

A stone hand-mill

work on. The upper stone was flat and circular and fitted on to the hollowed out, lower stone. It had a large hole in the centre while a wooden handle was inserted into a small hole near the outer edge.

Grinding was a heavy job. Two women sat facing on the ground. Both grasped the handle and set the upper stone spinning. They poured

Cooking bread on a metal dome.

Olive trees near the Mount of Olives.

A stone watchtower near Samaria.

When the widow of Zarapheth gathered sticks in order to make bread from her last bit of flour, and when Hosea called Ephraim 'an unturned cake', it was probably this kind of bread that was meant.[27] The barley loaves which Jesus used from a peasant boy's picnic to feed the five thousand were probably of the pitta bread variety.[28]

Barley was not only used for animal fodder but was eaten by the poor, for whom wheat was a luxury. When God tries to emphasise how he wants the very best for his people he says, 'I would feed you on pure wheat'.[29] Gideon was not a soldier and when God called him to deliver Israel he felt very inadequate. His confidence was boosted by the dream of one of the enemy soldiers in which a cake of barley flattened the camp. The inexperienced Gideon might feel as humble as barley bread but God showed him that he would accomplish his task successfully.[30]

Wild Figs

If bread was a dietary staple, so too were the fruits and vegetables which grow so prolifically in this part of the world. Amos gathered sycamore fruit; not the English sycamore but the like-sounding Hebrew *shiqmah*, or wild fig, which poor people used to eat.[31] It implies that Amos was either a poor man who supplemented his diet in this way or that he owned a wild fig orchard as many people did, king David included.[32]

Whichever way, the *shiqmah* is susceptible to frost. The psalmist knew this when he spoke of the frost which destroyed the sycamores in Egypt.[33] It will not grow above a certain altitude and Tekoa, where Amos lived, was in the Judaean highlands and well above its range. He must have travelled to lower ground to tend and collect its fruit.

The *shiqmah* serves many purposes. It still determines the demarcation line between the high ground of Upper Galilee, where it will not

Gathering grapes from vineyards in northern Israel.

grow, and Lower Galilee, where it is common. It was an easily obtained food for the poor whereas the proper fig was less available, being mostly a cultivated species. Its durable wood was also used for Egyptian mummy coffins.

The tree grows to about forty feet high, with horizontal branches starting low on the trunk. It was ideal for Zacchaeus to climb. This incident happened in spring, just before Jesus' last Passover. Even in sub-tropical Jericho the tree was probably not in full foliage. Zacchaeus only needed to climb a few feet up to get a good view.[34]

A Tower in a Vineyard

Grapes are another common dietary item, used fresh, dried or as wine. Vineyards are planted on terraced hillsides where the stony ground must be cleared before crops can grow. The smaller stones help to consolidate a surrounding hedge of thorns and cactus, grown to keep out wild animals. Bigger boulders are used to build a round watchtower, some twenty feet high. This gives shelter to the labourers who sleep there at the height of the season. It is also a vantage point to watch for robbers who try to steal the grapes. Somewhere close by is a stone trough for pressing out the grapes.

The big vineyards of Rishon Letzion and Zichron Yaacov in Israel today use every modern method. Go to the quieter hills of Samaria and vineyards as in Bible times are still seen with their crumbling terraces, thorny hedges and derelict watchtowers.[35]

The climax of a sordid tale occurred on the plain of Lebonah between Nablus and Shiloh. Certain men of the tribe of Benjamin had behaved despicably and the other tribes had sworn never again to give them their daughters in marriage. Already decimated, the tribe of Benjamin was dying out for lack of women. At this point the other tribes relented but, being unwilling to retract their vow, they had to seek another solution.

In those days, young girls dressed in white danced in the vineyards at the start and end of the grape harvest—on the 15th of Av in August and on the Day of Atonement in September. Young men customarily chose their brides from the dancers. In this case, the tribes agreed to let the men of Benjamin hide in the vineyards and seize the girls of their choice when they came out to dance.[36]

The Versatile Olive

The olive has always been one of the most valuable commodities of the Middle East. Although the berries are pickled for eating, it is the oil which is most important. It is used, amongst other things, medicinally, cosmetically, in cooking and for burning in the primitive, clay, wick lamps used before electric lights were invented. The story of Elisha and the widow shows its worth in the economy of those days.[37]

There is a story, surely apocryphal, to do with the wealth of the olive. Moses blessed the tribe of Asher saying, 'He shall dip his foot in oil'.[38] On these grounds, an American prospector decided that he would find oil somewhere in the land allocated to Asher. Not so! Asher's territory stretched along the coast from below Mount Carmel up into Lebanon and it included flourishing olive groves. Asher's wealth lay in olive oil, not crude. For that matter, had our prospector but understood Hebrew he could have saved his time. In Hebrew there is no ambiguity. Vegetable oil is *shemen*; crude is *neft*.

Olives ripen in September. The trees, which are not high, are beaten with rods to bring down the berries while young lads climb up to shake the top branches. The Torah forbade a second beating so as to leave something for the poor.[39] Isaiah foretold lean times when hardly any berries were left to be gleaned after the beating.[40]

Because it takes fifteen years before a young tree bears fruit, rather than grow new trees, the farmer gets fruit quickly by grafting from a cultivated olive tree onto a wild tree. It is significant, therefore, when Paul says that the Gentiles are a wild shoot which has been grafted on to Israel, the cultivated olive.

An olive press.

A horse-drawn olive press, with huge revolving millstone.

He knows that this is not the natural way of doing it and says so. He wants to show that the covenant promises have not been taken from Israel and transferred to the Gentiles, or to a Gentile church. Rather, the wild Gentile shoot has been brought in to join the cultivated tree of Israel in her already existing covenant relationship with God. Paul obviously feels that his illustration shows God's grace towards the Gentiles and emphasises both the primacy and permanency of his covenant with Israel.[41]

A Lodge in a Cucumber Patch

We cannot cover every aspect of agricultural life but we can pick out three further items.

Much of the countryside is totally without shade and to work in the sun at the height of summer is exhausting. Hammer four posts into the ground, rig up a rough roof of branches and sacking and, in a few minutes, you have a makeshift patch of shade. It is somewhere to eat and have a brief siesta when the sun is at its height. At the end of the day you leave it there, standing alone and conspicuous, until the winter gales demolish it. So, said Isaiah, would be Israel's fate when God had dealt with her for her sins.[42]

A Basket of Summer Fruits

The close of summer sees a bounty of fruits and vegetables stored for winter. When Amos had the vision of a basket of summer fruit, it must have contained some of the things we have just mentioned. There is an intended pun in this passage. In Hebrew, summer and summer fruit are both *qayitz*. Summer is the last stage of the agricultural cycle. Once the fruits are picked its end has come. Hence, the word for end is *qetz*. The prophet's meaning is clear in the Hebrew original. The basket of summer fruit portends that Israel's end is near and captivity looms.[43]

Trees of Field and Wood

Trees of the field bear edible fruit. Trees of the wood or forest do not. The prophets spoke of trees of the field, such as the fig, apple, plum or pomegranate, either yielding their fruit or languishing.[44] Also, a solitary apple tree amongst the trees of the wood illustrates the uniqueness of the beloved amongst all others in the eyes of the lover described in the Song of Songs.[45]

In contrast, men make an idol from a cedar or an oak which has grown amongst the trees of the forest.[46] Other people use the wood for fuel, either to give warmth or for cooking. In other words, they are careful to use a tree which does not produce edible fruit and which is, in that sense, expendable.

The Torah forbade destroying trees of the field in a siege.[47] Only the non-fruit bearing trees could be cut down or used to make siege engines and weapons. Fruit is food for both man and beast. Even in warfare, its value was recognised and it had to be protected, irrespective of whether the trees belonged to the enemy or not.

Bible references

1 Deuteronomy 22:10
  2 Corinthians 6:14 KJV
2 Matthew 11:29, 30
3 Luke 9:62
4 Acts 26:14
5 Mark 4:1–9
6 Matthew 13:24–30
7 Exodus 9:31, 32
8 1 Samuel 12:17
9 Deuteronomy 23:26
  Revelation 14:14–19
10 Deuteronomy 25:4
  1 Timothy 5:17, 18
11 Judges 6:11
12 Isaiah 41:14–16
13 2 Samuel 24:18–25

14 Isaiah 28:23–28 RSV
15 Matthew 7:4, 5
16 Psalm 1:4; Job 21:18
17 Luke 3:17
18 1 Kings 4:28 RSV
19 Proverbs 14:4
20 Exodus 5:12
21 Luke 6:38
22 Amos 9:9
23 Luke 22:31
24 Judges 16:21
25 Deuteronomy 24:6
26 Jeremiah 25:10
27 1 Kings 17:12; Hosea 7:8
28 John 6:9
29 Psalm 81:16
30 Judges 7:9–14
31 Amos 7:14

32 1 Chronicles 27:28
33 Psalm 78:47
34 Luke 19:1–10
35 Isaiah 5:1, 2; Mark 12:1
36 Judges 19—21
37 2 Kings 4:1–7
38 Deuteronomy 33:24
39 Deuteronomy 24:20
40 Isaiah 17:6
41 Romans 11:17–32
42 Isaiah 1:8
43 Amos 8:1, 2 RSV
44 Ezekiel 34:27 RSV; Joel 1:12
45 Song of Songs 2:3 RSV
46 Isaiah 44:14
47 Deuteronomy 20:19, 20

CHAPTER EIGHT

Cultural Ways Jesus Followed

We are all children of our own age and place and, unless we are taught differently, we will view the Bible from our own cultural perspective. Jesus, too, was thoroughly a child of his times, but how different they are from ours. How exciting and rewarding it is, therefore, to explore the common, daily life of the society in which he lived.

Home and Hospitality

Nomads and desert folks were tent dwellers but most people lived in simple, one roomed houses. Usually, the family animals slept at one end while the humans lived on a raised portion at the other. People did not need much furniture. When they were inside they sat cross-legged on the floor on woven rugs. In a peasant's house, the floor was of earth, perhaps covered with a rush carpet. Only the wealthy had flags and tiles.

In a hot country, no one stays indoors much and many domestic duties are performed outside. This is so even when the weather is cooler in winter. Any storms only last for a few days at a time and the sun always shines in between. Being higher in the sky at

that latitude, the sun is quite warm, even in winter. In summer, people probably did almost everything outside and only slept indoors.

Everyone slept together on thin sleeping mats which they rolled up during the day. The custom still obtains, even in some progressive villages. We can understand why Jesus said to a man, 'Take up your bed and walk'.[1] We can also appreciate why a certain householder grumbled about getting up for a late caller because, as he said, 'My children are in bed with me'.[2]

Stairs up an outside wall led to the flat roofs where a busy roof top culture existed and still does. The command to build a parapet around the roof makes good sense.[3] There Rahab hid two spies under some drying flax.[4] From such a vantage point David saw Bathsheba bathing in a normally concealed courtyard.[5] But was Bathsheba a little careless, maybe deliberately so? The woman of Shunem built a rooftop room for Elisha.[6]

Some men once made a hole in a roof and thereby brought a paralysed man to Jesus.[7] The Mishnah talks about passing fruit through a roof hatch. Did they enlarge something like this for their purposes? Roofs were only made of brushwood spread across beams and covered with mortar. They were easily broken and soon repaired.

Luke is the only gospel writer who talks about breaking up the tiles to get through the roof. This is strange as few roofs were tiled in that part of the world in those days. It probably reflects the fact that he was a Gentile who came from a place where tiled roofs were the norm. Neither was he one of the disciples who saw the incident for themselves. Certainly, Gentiles reading his gospel would more easily understand the event described.

Middle Eastern hospitality is a unique virtue. If, in desperation, a man comes to his enemy for food or asylum, the expectation is that he will be treated as an honoured guest. This explains why David found safety from Saul with his former enemies, the Philistines. He took a risk but the code of hospitality triumphed. Only later did he actually win the favour of the king.[8]

Rarely is hospitality abused. Why, then, did Jael kill Sisera when he fled to her tribe for protection in his defeat? After all, they were his allies. The reason is that he took advantage of her hospitality. He threatened her honour by entering the women's inner section of the tent where no men were allowed. He could be sure that not even his enemies would seek him there. The only way for Jael to prove her innocence and maintain her honour was to kill him.[9]

Greetings and Farewells

Greetings were, and still can be, both flowery and prolonged, as were farewells and other polite niceties of social intercourse. Over the centuries numerous formulae have developed to suit every occasion. Of course, the nice words are said by rote but they are important. As small a thing as serving a cup of coffee merits an exchange of good wishes between guest and host. The empty cup is returned with more mutual expressions of goodwill. In times of mourning or misfortune, however, some words are omitted or altered. It would never do to say, 'May things always be so for you' at such a time.

In the leisurely society of Jesus' day, time mattered even less than it does in the present Middle East. This is saying something. Every westerner knows the frustration of the response, 'Tomorrow', when he wants something right now. When people met friends or made new ones, they dropped other affairs and sat socialising for many hours.

This happened with a man who went to collect his runaway wife as told in Judges 19. He spent two days in farewell festivities with his father-in-law before he finally left for home.[10] When Jesus sent seventy disciples out on a mission he told them, 'Salute no one on the road'. He did not intend them to ignore everyone. Rather, they were not to waste time in the unprofitable chit chat of the prolonged, social occasion. Their task was too urgent.[11]

Inns and Travellers

Jesus expected the disciples to find hospitality during their mission with friends or sympathetic hearers. We know that he sometimes stayed with friends on his travels, such as Mary, Martha and Lazarus. He and his disciples must often have slept in the open but at times they would have been glad of shelter.

Courtyard of an old caravanserai or khan, Acco, similar to the inns of Bible times.

On main highways and in large villages, inns were plentiful and they are often mentioned in the Bible. They were quite different from a modern hotel. There is a good example of an eastern inn, though no longer working, near the harbour in Acco in Israel.

Inns consisted of a square of buildings set round a roomy courtyard. The lower storey was just a series of open alcoves where travellers stabled their animals for the night. Stairs led to an upper storey and a walkway which went round and overlooked the court on all four sides. The walkway gave access to more open recesses which provided sleeping quarters for the guests. In the centre of the courtyard was a well and troughs for watering the livestock. In the stable rooms were mangers for fodder. Baggage was stored in the open courtyard and, in the case of a rich man or merchant, there would be a servant on guard to protect it.

Travellers carried provisions for themselves and their beasts and did their own chores. There was no privacy and strangers bedded down on their own sleeping mats together. The inn keeper took the money and kept things in order. He had no call to serve his guests except in a general way although, for a fee, he might agree to undertake specific duties. The good Samaritan paid the inn keeper to care for the wounded man.[12]

Mary and Joseph found no room in the Bethlehem inn and finally took shelter in what we fondly assume to be a stable. Luke, who records the incident, merely says that Mary laid her baby in a manger. From that statement we deduce that the manger was in a stable.

Did this mean that the upper storey rooms of the inn were full and that they slept with the animals below? Quite likely! We tend to imagine them finding a cosy shed belonging to a kind householder. This too is possible; except that the shed would be a crude, stone affair, almost certainly cramped, dark, smelly and draughty. It might even have been a cave. Caves are common in hilly limestone country and people have always utilised them for their own purposes. We greatly idealise these stories. The reality was less pleasant.

Sitting in the Gate

The social and administrative centre of any sizeable community was the city gate although, even if a place was not walled, it still had elders who were responsible for the proper running of affairs. Large towns were walled and immediately inside the gates was an open area which was the town business centre. This was the place for public assembly, to seek justice, spread news or negotiate business. Each day the city elders sat there and dealt with any issues which members of the public brought before them.

The gates were also part of the defence system. Excavations of places like Megiddo, in Israel, show how elaborately designed some were in order to make it difficult for enemies to enter. They were constructed with a series of right-angled turns in order to prevent high speed charges from horses and chariots. Everywhere were vantage points from which soldiers could defend against attack.

Abraham bargained with the Hittites in the city gate when he bought Sarah's burial cave.[13] Boaz negotiated with his relative in the gate for the right to marry Ruth.[14] Here Absalom paved the way for his rebellion against his father.[15] Job sat there regularly, esteemed by all, until illness laid him aside.[16] Jesus talked

about the needle's eye.[17] This is said to be a small doorway set in the large main gates.

The massive gates were closed at sundown, as a security measure. A late traveller could be vetted and allowed to enter this way if the sentry approved, but nothing else. The space was too small for animals and baggage. Bear in mind that donkeys were used as local beasts of burden but camels were more suitable for carrying large loads for long distances and across sandy terrain. An unladen donkey might just get through the eye of the needle. A camel, loaded or unloaded, could only enter when the main gates were open. The same applied to a chariot or war horse.

The approach to Jerusalem's Lion Gate.

Market inside the Damascus Gate, Jerusalem.

Business in the Bazaars

The bazaar is the shopping centre of a town. It is a tangle of alleys filled with colourful wares, noise and bustle by day and deserted once darkness falls. Shops and work places open directly on to the lanes by way of wide archways which are shuttered at night. Shopkeepers display their goods in the open while craftsmen work on the street in front of their shops.

It was, and is, customary to barter. The buyer offers a low sum for such, in his opinion, shoddy goods. The merchant asks an exorbitant price for his quality wares. Eventually, after much spirited negotiation,

they reach a happy medium and the sale is made. It seems that, in his grief, Abraham had no heart to haggle when he bought Sarah's burial plot but paid the top asking price. The start of the procedure is still familiar.

At first, Ephron said what Middle Eastern salesmen still say, "For you, nothing! It's a gift'.[18] Everyone knows, as did Abraham, that this is not to be taken seriously. It does, however, emphasise the significance of Isaiah's call to those who are thirsty to come and buy water without price.[19] Here the offer of something for nothing is genuine. Buying water sounds strange to western ears but in the bazaars, water sellers were as common as the man who goes round today with a tray, glasses and a jug, selling mint tea or lemonade.

Each street is devoted to one kind of business. For instance, when Jeremiah visited a potter, he went to the street of the potters where the man both worked and lived behind the shop.[20] While Jeremiah was in prison, the king gave him a loaf of bread each day from the street of the bakers.[21] Was there a street of the carpenters in the Nazareth bazaar, where Joseph and his family lived behind the shop?

Paul supported himself and his companions throughout his ministry by making tents.[22] He worked in Corinth with Aquila and Priscilla who were also tent makers, no doubt in a workshop in the street of the tent makers.[23] If he stayed some time in a place, did he rent his own premises where he lived and practised his trade?

Bazaar lanes are too narrow for cars and may be stepped. Men with hand carts and laden donkeys bring in the wares and, in a few places, there is still the burden bearer. His only aid is a five yard rope but with it he carries weights which would crush him if he fell. He crouches before a load, skilfully twists his rope around it without any knots, then suddenly lifts with an exhalation of breath; as weightlifters and hard-hitting tennis players do, to prevent bursting a blood vessel.

A friend once saw a man carry a piano in this way. The load balances across the shoulders, bowing the bearer down. A big pack juts forward over his head so that he cannot see before him and must shout to clear his way. Archaeologists have discovered ancient sculptures of burden bearers and many references to them occur in the Bible.

When Nehemiah rebuilt the walls of Jerusalem, there was so much rubble to move that the strength of the carriers began to fail.[24] The psalmist was overwhelmed with guilt, like a huge burden pressing over his head.[25] Jesus compared the Oral Torah which the scribes and Pharisees imposed on the people with a heavy burden which they refused to alleviate.[26]

If a porter is tired, he asks a passer-by to stoop under his load and take the weight for a moment rather than put his burden down. This image underlies the words, 'Bear each other's burdens'. The Greek term is *baros*. It means a very heavy load. Each person is then told to carry his own burden. Here the Greek word is *phortion*, something light which is carried by hand.[27] We must neither underestimate someone else's suffering nor overestimate our own minor hardships.

Until the advent of modern materials, ropes were made from vegetable matter. We do not know what the ropes of the burden bearers came from but there is an interesting bush which grows on the coastal plain and in the Negev. Its fibres make exceedingly strong ropes. It is called the *thymelea hirsuta* or, in Hebrew, the *yitran*. From this comes the word *yeter*, meaning the guy rope of a tent.

To make a rope, the bark is peeled off and the fibrous strands are separated then twisted or plaited. Such a cable can pull a jeep out of deep mud and hold a half ton weight. Survival courses in Israel teach how to recognise and use this plant. The bush is easily found and, despite the fact that the sap irritates and smells unpleasant, people have utilised its fibres for thousands of years. Significantly, the *yitran* fibres are strongest when they are still moist.

It is mentioned once in the Bible in a verse that is hard to translate meaningfully in western terms. As Delilah probes the secret of Samson's strength, he tells her to tie him with seven new bowstrings, *yetarim*, which have not been dried.[28] The King James Bible calls them withs (withes), which is the nearest that any version gets to a reasonable translation. Withes are the flexible hazel twigs used for weaving baskets and binding things.

Office of the Forerunner

In Middle Eastern countries the forerunner is still a familiar figure. Although he is seen less frequently in Jerusalem today, he sometimes accompanies a high church dignitary on a ceremonial procession through the streets. It is his job to run before his master, to clear the way along narrow, crowded streets, to open doors and announce his master's coming and to wait upon him when he arrives.

The forerunner is resplendently dressed. Beneath a short, white tunic whose wide sleeves billow as he moves, his legs are bare for running. He has an embroidered waistcoat, a bright scarf around his waist and a rod which he uses freely on anyone who impedes his way. In open country he can easily run for at least twelve miles before a horse drawn carriage.

Samuel warned Israel that their new king would take their sons to be, amongst other things, his forerunners.[29] Both Absalom and Adonijah took fifty men to run before their chariots in their bids for the throne.[30] We see how fit Elijah was when he ran from Carmel to Jezreel before Ahab's retinue; some twenty miles in pouring rain.[31] We can only guess why he chose to act as Ahab's forerunner on that occasion. Was it to show everyone for miles around that if he was restored to the king's favour, it had to be his God, the Lord, who had broken the long drought and not Baal?

The prophet foretold that Elijah would be the Messiah's forerunner.[32] Jesus confirmed that John the Baptist, who had come in the spirit and power of Elijah, fulfilled that office.[33] There is, however, a deeper significance in this prophecy. Elijah and Moses appeared at the Transfiguration and some commentators hold that they are the two, unidentified witnesses of the book of Revelation who will precede the second coming.[34]

Meanwhile, Jesus has already entered heaven as our forerunner.[35] This does not mean that he has simply got there first before us. It rather shows his humility and care for us. By his saving work, he has taken it upon himself to clear the way ahead and open the door into heaven for all who will follow behind him. In

Part of the busy Arab bazaar inside the Old City of Jerusalem.

heaven he will personally present to the Father the mortal beings he came to save.

Life with the Romans

The Romans took control of the region which they called Palestine, the century before Jesus. After Herod the Great, they divided the country under the charge of certain of his descendants. They were responsible for local affairs but were politically answerable to Rome and likely to be deposed if their policies did not meet with approval.

Roman soldiers were stationed everywhere. No doubt most were tough but decent enough chaps, like the centurion who built the synagogue in Capernaum and Cornelius who tried to live righteously. At the same time, the Romans were cruel and tolerated no defiance. Notwithstanding, as long as people paid their taxes they were, in principle, allowed to live as they pleased. Of course, many Roman soldiers misused their position and all systems get abused. We see examples of this in the Bible.

Some soldiers coerced the local people into fetching and carrying for them. They commandeered any commodity which they desired and were physically abusive if their demands were resisted. This may have been what Jesus was referring to when he talked about going the second mile, turning the other cheek, giving a cloak in addition to a coat and loving one's enemies and persecutors.[36] John the Baptist must also have had these things in mind when he told the soldiers, 'No intimidation! No extortion!'[37]

The reconstructed Roman amphitheatre at Caesarea Maritima.

The Romans appointed local Jews as tax collectors and their own nation considered them to be collaborators and traitors. It was acceptable for them to realise some financial benefit from their job but people resented the exorbitant profits they made at their expense. John the Baptist cautioned the tax collectors who came for baptism, 'Exact no more than your rate!'[38]

Zacchaeus had done well for himself as a senior tax collector. He offered to repay four times the amount to anyone he had defrauded, which was almost the maximum amount for restitution stipulated in the Torah.[39] He also determined to give half his assets to the poor.[40] Tax collectors were clever, educated and rich men. Materially, Matthew and Zacchaeus gave up a lot to follow Jesus.

Broadly speaking there were three attitudes to Rome within the country. The Zealots were extreme nationalists who advocated force against the occupying power. The fervour of some cost them their lives by crucifixion, for Rome clamped down severely on any opposition. One of the disciples was a Zealot.[41]

At the other end of the spectrum were the Sadducees. They were the wealthy aristocracy and upper class priests who did all they could to keep in with Rome and avoid confrontation. In the centre were the ordinary people, the lower class priests and the Pharisees. Although they hated their foreign overlords, the most important thing was that they could practise their religion in their own way.

The Romans kept charge of the High Priest's robes as a guarantee of national co-operation. The garrison fortress of Antonia overlooked the inner courts of the Temple. As the attempt to lynch Paul shows, the soldiers were on the spot the moment there was any trouble.[42] It was humiliating but such insults were the price for religious freedom. As such they were bearable.

Ordinary folks concentrated on daily survival in a hard world. Their great comfort was their hope in the imminent arrival of a leader who would free them from foreign subjugation and restore their national sovereignty. Into this climate of spiritual optimism came Jesus. He won the allegiance of all those whose minds were open enough to assimilate the new interpretations of the messianic kingdom which he propounded.

Bible references

		15 2 Samuel 15:2	31 1 Kings 18:45, 46
		16 Job 29:7	32 Malachi 4:5, 6
1	Mark 2:9	17 Mark 10:25	33 Matthew 11:11–14
2	Luke 11:7 RSV	18 Genesis 23:7–16	Luke 1:16, 17
3	Deuteronomy 22:8	19 Isaiah 55:1–3	34 Luke 9:28–36
4	Joshua 2:6	20 Jeremiah 18:1–5	Revelation 11:3
5	2 Samuel 11:2	21 Jeremiah 37:21	35 Hebrews 6:20 RSV
6	2 Kings 4:10	22 2 Thessalonians 3:7, 8	36 Matthew 5:38–48
7	Luke 5:19	23 Acts 18:1–4	37 Luke 3:14
8	1 Samuel 27:29	24 Nehemiah 4:4 RSV	38 Luke 3:13
9	Judges 4:17–22	25 Psalm 38:4 RSV	39 Exodus 22:1 RSV
10	Judges 19:1–9	26 Matthew 23:4;11:30	40 Luke 19:8
11	Luke 10:4	27 Galatians 6:2, 5 RSV	41 Luke 6:15
12	Luke 10:35	28 Judges 16:7	42 Acts 21:31
13	Genesis 23:18 RSV	29 1 Samuel 8:11	
14	Ruth 4:1	30 2 Samuel 15:1; 1 Kings 1:5	

CHAPTER NINE

Religious Customs Jesus Kept

The precepts of Judaism permeate every realm of a devout Jewish person's life. The sacred and secular are inseparable as the whole daily routine is lived out in the light of Torah; Oral Torah in particular. It was the same in Jesus' day. Food, ablutions, speech, sex and much more were all regulated, no less than the religious duties of prayer and fasting.

At best, the system inculcated upright and disciplined behaviour. Jesus recognised this when he told people to follow the teaching of the scribes and Pharisees. In the same breath, however, he also warned against copying their behaviour. Sadly, many of them did not always practise what they preached and brought the Torah into disrepute by the way they manipulated it.[1] We see examples of this as we examine the main areas of involvement below.

Orthodox Jews pray at the Tomb of the Patriarchs, Hebron.

Foods, Fit and Unfit

Kashrut, the Jewish food law system, comes from a root *k-sh-r* meaning fit. Fit, in this case, means ritually suitable for eating. Although health and hygiene are part of the underlying rationale, the idea that *kosher* means clean is wrong. The whole biblical system is set out in Leviticus 11 and Deuteronomy 14:15–21. These chapters define the birds and animals which are allowed or disallowed as food.

Some things are abhorrent, such as insects and reptiles. Often there is something dangerous to health about them as with birds or animals which eat carrion. Some animals and customs were associated with idolatry, as may have been the case with the pig and the prohibition against boiling a kid in its mother's milk.[2] Because of this, milk and meat products are nowadays kept totally separate and are never stored, prepared or eaten together.

Certain fatty parts of an animal were burned on the altar and were not to be eaten.[3] God condemned Eli's sons for taking the fat from the sacrifices for themselves.[4] Sacrifice has long ceased but suet is still not kosher. Because blood represents the life force it is also forbidden. The method of ritual slaughter, which allows blood to drain away, evolves from this rule.[5] Saul's soldiers were so ravenous after a long battle that they flouted this command.[6]

Did Jesus Keep Kashrut?

The evidence suggests that Jesus did keep *kashrut* although we must bear in mind two things. Ordinary people did not necessarily follow all the meticulous regulations of the Pharisees and *kashrut* is more complicated now than it was then. Jesus came from a religious home where, as we have already seen, the Torah was carefully observed.

The fact that he ate with tax gatherers and sinners does not imply that the food was not kosher. These people were Jews. Their standards of *kashrut* may not have been acceptable to the strict religious groups but very few people could meet their standards. It seems that the disapproval of the critics was directed against the company Jesus kept rather than the food that his friends served.[7]

Presumably the disciples also went to the party that Matthew gave to introduce his friends to Jesus. However, whether they were present or not, they could not have lived so closely with him without eating regularly together. This is an important point. When Peter had his vision of the unclean animals he said emphatically, 'I have never eaten anything unclean in my life'.[8] Peter had three close years with Jesus. If he could make such a claim, surely Jesus could too.

As some of the Jewish religious authorities delighted in trying to catch Jesus out, it is unlikely that they would have missed any lapse in his eating habits. Is it not significant, then, that the gospels record no such criticism? Even the complaint that he and the disciples ate without washing their hands has to do with ritual cleanness, not with *kashrut*.

What, then, is the meaning of the statement 'thus he declared all foods clean'? Does this not imply that Jesus was doing away with the food laws at this point? Note that it was made in connection with his teaching that a man is defiled by the evil that comes out of him and not by the food that goes into him.[9] Jesus was

An orthodox Jew checks the *kashrut* of a citrus (*etrog*) before the *Succot* festival.

simply propounding the spiritual principle that what people are, and what they say and do, is more important than the kind of food they eat.

Ceremonial Uncleanness

Ritual uncleanness has nothing to do with hygiene. It is an ancient, widely practised, religious classification which renders a person unfit to take part in the rites of the cult. For Judaism this meant the Temple ceremonial.

The condition of ritual uncleanness symbol-ises a perceived religious reality. The god is above and beyond the beings who offer him their allegiance but who are unworthy to relate to him in any way. Different religions try to bridge the gap and make the unacceptable acceptable to the deity in differing ways. In many it involves a combination of sacrifice and ritual ablution. In Judaism, ritual impurity symbolises sin, for it is sin which separates mankind from a holy God. Sacrifice and wash-ing typify both the need for, and the possibility of, expiation and cleansing from sin.

The New Testament teaches that washing and sacrifice are external symbols of how to deal with an inward condition. Sin is not just wrong action. It is an innate state of human nature. Before we can acceptably draw near to God, the very ground of our being must be transformed. Thus, sacrifice and washing are linked to the concept of a purified conscience.

Such a fundamental achievement cannot be accomplished by sprinkling a person with the blood of bulls and goats or the ashes of a heifer. (This reference to ashes is connected to the rite of the red heifer, which we examine shortly.) A purified conscience is obtained only through the blood of Jesus and the work of the Holy Spirit within our hearts.[10]

Causes of Uncleanness

Two of the most common causes of ritual impurity were childbirth and menstruation. Menstrual blood was especially defiling and a menstruating woman transmitted ritual uncleanness to all she touched.

Did Laban guess that Rachel was guilty when he sought his missing gods in her tent? She sat on the camel litter, where they were hidden, and excused herself from rising because she claimed to have a period. Whether she did or not, Laban did not risk contracting ritual impurity and left the litter unsearched. Moreover, if she had stolen his gods, he surely preferred not to know since Jacob had sworn to put the thief to death.[11]

The woman who touched the hem of Jesus' robe had permanent bleeding. The extreme ritual contagiousness of her state highlights the enormity of her act in grasping the fringes of the prayer shawl, the most holy part of a holy man's clothes.[12]

Producing and being touched by semen or spitting on someone are other causes of uncleanness.[13] Leprosy was also held to be a state of impurity. After Miriam criticised Moses and became temporarily leprous, she was separated from the community for a week. In her case, however, the grounds were that if her father had only spat at her, she would have been unclean for that time.[14] This shows what indignity Jesus endured when those who tried him spat at him.

There were many lesser causes of ritual impurity, some according to the traditions of men rather than the Bible. The priests, for instance, felt that even to go into the praetorium for the trial of Jesus would defile them. Jews did not associate with Gentiles for the same reason.

Cleansing through the *Mikveh*

Purification for lesser defilement centred round the *mikveh* or ritual bath. A *mikveh* means a place where water gathers. Whether it is a hole in the ground or a modern, tiled and heated affair, it must link to a natural, running, water supply, like a stream or spring.

The *mikveh* was, and is, an important adjunct to daily life. Orthodox communities will build one before a synagogue.

In Bible days both men and women practised immersion regularly. After any contact with impurity, a person took the ritual bath, changed clothes and was clean at sunset.[15] No one could enter the Temple precincts without first immersing in a *mikveh*. Mary, going to the Temple for her purification after Jesus' birth, must have done so. Religious women still go to a *mikveh* every month, totally covering their bodies in the water. That this is a ritual act is clearly implied by the fact that they have a proper bath beforehand.

Within the last twenty years, archaeologists have uncovered a huge complex of ritual baths outside the excavated remains of the main entrance to the Temple. There are enough baths to have served the pilgrim crowds who inundated Jerusalem during the festivals as well as the regular, local visitors throughout the year.

When Peter refused to let Jesus wash his feet before the Last Supper, Jesus replied, 'If I do not wash you, you have no part in me'. Peter then wanted everything done, hands and head included. Jesus responded, 'He who has bathed . . . is clean all over'. In other words, they had all just been through the *mikveh* before the Passover meal and were ritually clean.[16]

What did need washing was their feet. Apparently, nobody was willing to do this for the others. Jesus was not concerned with ritual purity at that moment. He was teaching a needed lesson on humility and service, for it was the duty of the lowest slave to wash feet, not the master of the house.

Sprinkling the Ashes of the Red Heifer[17]

The greatest degree of defilement derived from touching a dead body. What an impression it must have made on everyone when Jesus raised to life the son of the widow of Nain and took him by the hand. Corpse defilement was only removed by one specific remedy; sprinkling with water into which were stirred the ashes obtained from burning a red heifer. *Parah*, the rabbinic treatise of the Mishnah which describes this custom, tells us many interesting things. We can mention only a few here.

A red-haired cow was killed and, with many meticulous rituals, its carcase was burned outside the city on the Mount of Olives. The ashes were then divided into three and stored separately. A cow that met the strict specifications of the rabbis was rare but the ashes were used so sparingly that they lasted a long time. *Parah* tells how only seven (some say nine) beasts were used during all of the two Temple periods.

People who had touched a corpse were unclean for seven days, or until such time as they could observe the necessary cleansing rituals. On the third day, a clean person sprinkled the unclean one with a bunch of hyssop dipped in water containing a tiny amount of the ash. On the seventh day they were sprinkled again. They then immersed in a *mikveh*, changed their clothes and were clean at sunset.

Jars of lustral water, as it is sometimes

Remains of an ancient Jewish *mikveh*, or ritual bath, at Modiin, Israel.

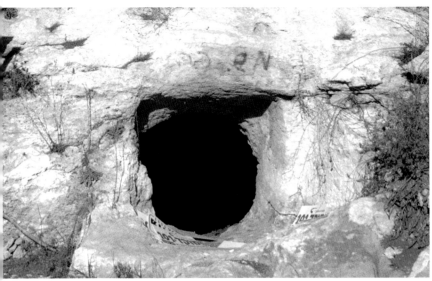

termed, were apparently set in wall niches in public places in Jerusalem. The Mishnah says that the ground below was slippery 'because of the much water that was sprinkled there'. If Jesus touched dead bodies, we must assume that he and his disciples knew all about the rituals of the red heifer and observed them before ever they entered the Temple.

Did David refer to this same custom, or something similar, when he grieved over his sin of adultery saying, 'Purge me with hyssop and I shall be clean'?[18] There is no great mystery over the use of hyssop in any of the religious rituals which we read about in the Bible. It was a common, bushy plant which easily absorbed liquids. This is why they offered Jesus, when he was on the cross, a drink from a bunch of hyssop held to his mouth.

There is a puzzle about the red heifer which the rabbis recognise but cannot solve. At one and the same time, it both defiles the clean and purifies the unclean. The priests who prepared it were made unclean, although the *mikveh* and a change of clothes were sufficient for their cleansing. The defiled who were sprinkled with its ashes were made pure.

Only as we see the fulfilment of its typology in Jesus can we offer a solution to the puzzle. Jesus suffered outside the city. In his suffering he, the sinless one, became sin in order to purify sinners and bring them acceptably to a holy God.[19]

Vows and Oaths

Jesus deplored the way that the Oral Torah sometimes took precedence over the Written Torah. For example, the Torah said that one must honour one's parents. Some people,

however, dedicated part of their means to God and then told their parents that they could no longer help them.[20] Underlying such behaviour was a system of making vows and oaths. A treatise of the Mishnah, *Nedarim* or Vows, explains how matters worked.

For instance, a man might swear that he would take no benefit from his friend. From then on, no borrowing, lending, buying or selling could take place between them. If the man who had made the vow had no food, he could not accept some from his friend, even if it were offered. A way round was for the friend to give food to a third man as a gift. The third party was allowed to give it to the man under vow who would then be free to eat it.

People used various forms of speech to make vows. They might say, 'By the *korban*', which was one of the sacrifices, or 'By the altar' and 'By Jerusalem'.[21] A slight change in wording could make what sounded like a vow to be not so. A carelessly worded, casual statement might actually prove to be a vow which committed a person to a course of action they had not intended.

The scandal lay in the fact that there were ways of getting out of inconvenient vows whereas, if the vow was advantageous, a person did not seek dispensation even if it were possible. No wonder that even for a binding promise, Jesus advocated the integrity of a plain yes or no.[22] The abuse of vows was widespread, silly, damaging and dishonest. Jesus condemned them.

Nedarim tells the story of a father and son who quarrelled. The son angrily vowed that his father would receive no more benefit from him. This precluded him from visiting his son's home and eating there. The time came for the wedding of the grandson and they wanted the old man to attend the festivities held in their home. Unfortunately, this was forbidden. The son solved the problem by giving his courtyard and the banquet to a friend as a gift. The friend promptly said, 'If they are mine they are dedicated to heaven'. In this way he pre-empted anyone from receiving any further benefit from them. We are not told what happened next. Was it the end of the party and of the friendship or did they find a way to revoke the vows and start again?

Nazirite Vows

We do not know why people took nazirite vows. They entailed much self discipline as the person concerned consumed nothing deriving from the grape, did not cut his hair and was not to touch a dead body.[23] Women also became nazirites but less frequently than men.

Men such as Samson, Samuel and John the Baptist, had to be nazirites from birth. In other words, even before they were born, God had set them aside for a special task. In childhood, their parents were responsible for preserving their nazirite status. As adults they had to do so for themselves. We know that Samson failed in this respect. Significantly, when Delilah cut his hair, his phenomenal strength left him and only returned as it grew again.

Others, like Paul, took a voluntary nazirite vow for a set time. At the end of the period they made sacrifices in the Temple and cut their hair in a room set aside for that purpose.[24] Does the nazirite vow typify the total consecration, even to the point of self denial, that God expects from those who wish to serve him?

Good Deeds

The rabbis say that there are six hundred and thirteen commandments or *mitzvot* in the Torah. Two hundred and forty-eight are positive and three hundred and sixty-five are negative. Those to do with the Temple can no longer be obeyed but others are still binding upon Jewish people. Today, a *mitzvah* is often loosely defined as a good deed or any kind act.

Three *mitzvot* are especially meritorious; prayer, fasting and charity. It was not by accident that Jesus dealt at some length with these three topics in his teaching.[25] Prayer is such a big subject that we deal with it in a separate chapter. At this stage it is enough to point out that Jesus did not say, 'If you pray' but, 'When you pray'. Prayer was part of the religious culture of the day, for sinner as well as saint, according to the story of the tax collector and the Pharisee.[26]

Fasting

Fasting, too, was part of life for people from all levels of society. A small tractate of the Mishnah, called *Taanit*, covers the subject. *Taanit* means affliction and, in Judaism, a fast is much more than abstinence from food. It is a time to afflict the soul.

It was easy to tell if people were fasting. They abstained from food and drink and went barefoot. They did not wash or anoint themselves with the sweet oils which it was the custom to put on the head and skin, much as we use scent and creams. Today Jewish people wear canvas shoes or thick socks and do not use cosmetics. Lastly, they did not have sexual intercourse. According to Jesus, they also pulled long, gloomy faces.[27]

How accurately the gospels describe the customs of the day. John the Baptist's disciples fasted often. So did the Pharisees. They could not understand why Jesus' followers did not.[28] Jesus also fasted before he began his ministry and he knew that a time would come when his own disciples would need to fast. What he did insist upon was that the purpose of fasting is not a public display of asceticism but a private self discipline before God.[29]

Appropriately enough for a country where drought is always a hazard, much of *Taanit* shows how fasting was regulated in response to insufficient rainfall. Apart from this, we learn that the second and fifth days of the Jewish week (Monday and Thursday) were regular fast days. This is because these days were market days and public, religious fasts were officially held at market and in the open market place. Those who fasted there were very much on display. Did the Pharisee who boasted that he fasted twice a week do so on these occasions?[30]

The anniversary of a national calamity often became a public fast, as happened after the destruction of the first Temple.[31] The fasts in this passage in Zechariah commemorate the following events associated with the tragedy.

In the fourth month, the Babylonians breached the walls of Jerusalem. Three weeks later, in the fifth, they destroyed the Temple. A year or two later, in the seventh month, Gedaliah, the governor of the land appointed by the Babylonians, was murdered.[32] The fast of the tenth month goes back to when the Babylonians first began to besiege Jerusalem. The siege itself lasted a year and a half before they finally managed to breach the walls. In the messianic age, these fasts will become feasts but, to this day, they still remain fasts.

Charity

In the women's courtyard in the Temple stood thirteen money boxes called trumpets because of their shape. Each had a set purpose and one trumpet was for charitable donations. Here the widow put her two coins which, from Jesus' perspective, outweighed all the contributions of the rich.[33]

It was the custom for the wealthy to sound a trumpet ahead of them to announce that they were handing out gifts. It called the poor to come and receive but it was also a way of parading their generosity which Jesus condemned. All who heard him grasped the punning of the trumpet reference.[34]

The Hebrew for charity, *tzedaqah*, is also the regular word for righteousness. By implication, to be righteous may be many things but, above all, it is to be charitable. Jewish people are very generous and support many charitable causes, so it comes as a surprise to visit a modern Israeli city like Tel Aviv and see Jewish beggars.

Some beggars are genuinely needy and Judaism accepts that the poor have a right to be cared for. Others are what one might call professional beggars. The professional beggar is an essential part of Jewish religious life. He, for such a one is usually a man, gives the wealthy a means of being righteous.

The main reason for this goes back to the loss of the Temple and the cessation of the blood sacrifices which atoned for sin. One thing which is now believed to atone for sin is prayer, or the service of the heart. Fasting is another, which is why the great fast of the Day of Atonement is so important. The third great pillar of atonement is charity.

If you visit the religious quarter of any city in Israel, or go to towns like Tiberias or Bnei Brak which have a strong religious tradition, you will see professional beggars. This is seen as an honourable trade. Stories are told, no doubt true, of Jewish mendicants who have lived in luxury and died wealthy men in this way.

Any act of charity not only helps to atone for sin, it also adds to a store of merit, or righteousness, being accumulated in the donor's favour. It is one of the most important *mitzvot* in Judaism and, like prayer and fasting, was a normal part of daily New Testament life.

Bible references

1   Matthew 23:1–3
2   Exodus 23:19
3   Leviticus 3:17
4   1 Samuel 2:12–17
5   Leviticus 17:10–14
6   1 Samuel 14:32
7   Luke 5:30
8   Acts 10:14
9   Mark 7:14–22
10 Hebrews 9:9–14
11 Genesis 31:32–35
12 Luke 8:44
13 Leviticus 15:16–18
14 Numbers 12:14
15 Leviticus 15:5 *et al*
16 John 13:5–15
17 Numbers 19
18 Psalm 51:7
19 2 Corinthians 5:21
20 Mark 7:9–13
21 Matthew 23:16–22
22 Matthew 5:33–37
23 Numbers 6:1–8
24 Acts 18:18; 21:23
25 Matthew 6:1–18
26 Luke 18:9–14
27 Matthew 6:16–18
28 Luke 5:33
29 Matthew 6:16–18
30 Luke 18:12
31 Zechariah 7:3–5; 8:18, 19
32 Jeremiah 41:2
33 Luke 21:1–4
34 Matthew 6:2

CHAPTER TEN

Festivals Jesus Celebrated

S.R. Hirsch, a Jewish scholar, once said, 'The catechism of the Jew is his calendar'. The calendar was ordained by God between three and four thousand years ago. It is outlined in Leviticus 23 and Numbers 28 and 29. Although it is based on the agricultural seasons of the year, just as were the calendars of other nations, the festivities were removed from the realm of the idolatrous and given a new meaning which set them apart from other systems.

The Jewish year offers Israel a perpetual reminder of God's intervention into human history which established Israel as a nation. Each season is linked to some act of divine control which shaped the theology of the Jewish people for all time. Each feast and fast encapsulates some aspect of Jewish belief and ideals.

The Three Pilgrim Festivals

God commanded that Israel's males worship three times a year at the place where he had 'set his name'.[1] Once the Temple was built, this meant Jerusalem. The Pilgrim Festivals, as these occasions were called, were Passover in April, Pentecost in June and Tabernacles in late September or early October. At these times the people presented their tithes, firstfruits and freewill gifts to God in either kind or money. The gifts helped to maintain the Temple and the priesthood.

There were other feasts in addition to the Pilgrim Festivals. All of them were celebrated in the Temple with a pageantry unhinted at by the gospel writers. They had no need to describe these things. Everyone knew. They wisely concentrated on the actions and teaching of Jesus which were relevant to the truths they wanted to expound. Few readers now know this background so we turn to the rabbinic records to supply it for us.

Preparing for a Festival

Before important events, gangs of workmen tidied up the roads leading to Jerusalem. If it was just after the winter rains, as at Passover, the dirt tracks were rutted and even paved roads needed attention. Similar preparations of straightening, smoothing, banking up and preparing the highway, be they in a real or in metaphorical sense, will precede the coming of the Messiah to Jerusalem.[2]

In some places along the roadside were tombs of holy men. Though venerated, they still carried the contagious taint of corpse

The Jewish Festivals

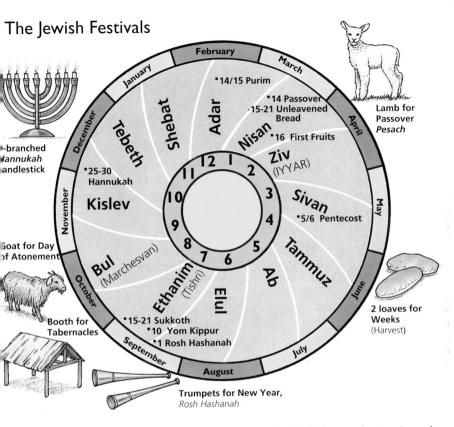

9-branched Hannukah candlestick

Lamb for Passover
Pesach

Goat for Day of Atonement

Booth for Tabernacles

2 loaves for Weeks (Harvest)

Trumpets for New Year, *Rosh Hashanah*

Months and festivals (inner calendar):

- December — Tebeth
- January — Shebat
- February — Adar
  - •14/15 Purim
- March — Nisan
  - •14 Passover
  - •15-21 Unleavened Bread
  - •16 First Fruits
- April — Ziv (IYYAR)
- May — Sivan
  - •5/6 Pentecost
- June — Tammuz
- July — Ab
- August — Elul
- September — Ethanim (Tishri)
  - •15-21 Sukkoth
  - •10 Yom Kippur
  - •1 Rosh Hashanah
- October — Bul (Marchesvan)
- November — Kislev
  - •25-30 Hannukah

defilement which no pilgrim wished to incur. The workmen whitewashed the tombs to warn the pilgrims away. They looked attractive and had a religious significance but they were to be avoided. What condemnation it was when Jesus compared the Pharisees to these same whitewashed sepulchres.[3]

The nearer Jerusalem, the greater the crowds of travellers. The Talmud tells that Agrippa I, king of Judaea 41–44 CE, once ordered a census by removing and counting the kidneys from the Passover lambs. There were six hundred thousand pairs. As each lamb supplied an extended family unit, probably of at least twelve people, it is hard to imagine the throngs crushing into the city. The code of hospitality decreed that Jerusalemites and neighbouring villagers opened their homes to friend and stranger on these occasions but many must have slept in the open outside the city.

Most pilgrims were either Jews or proselyte converts to Judaism. They came, not only from Judaea and Galilee, but from all over the diaspora which stretched from Babylonia to countries around the Mediterranean seaboard and beyond.

Jews living locally would visit Jerusalem regularly, provided they could afford the time for the journey. The gospels show that Jesus and his disciples went up for most of the big festivals. Diaspora Jews might manage the trip once in a lifetime and great was their excitement as they approached Jerusalem. Psalms 120 to 134 are called the Songs of Ascents. Traditionally the pilgrims started to sing them as they came in sight of the city. The last Psalms were sung in the precincts of the Temple itself.

Passover or Pesach

Many churches organise Passover demonstrations to show the origin of the communion service in the last supper. Plenty is written on this elsewhere which we shall not duplicate. The one issue we shall deal with here is the apparent discrepancy between the synoptic gospels (the first three) and John regarding the time when Jesus held the Last Supper.

The Time of the Last Supper
According to Matthew, Mark and Luke, Jesus shared the Passover meal, or *seder*, with his disciples on the Thursday evening. He was crucified on Friday morning and rose on Sunday morning, the first day of the week. In John's gospel, we might assume that the final meal which Jesus shared with his disciples was also the normal Passover *seder* until we come to a certain event at his trial.

The problem is found in Jesus' appearance before Pilate. John tells us that the priests would not enter the court room lest they be ritually defiled and therefore unable to eat the Passover.[4] This suggests that Jesus must have had his Passover meal a day early, if the priests were only expecting to hold it on the Friday evening. There are a few possible explanations for this discrepancy.

Although the religious leaders were most careful in determining the appearance of the new moon, and hence the exact days on which any festival would fall in that month, they did sometimes disagree. In such a case, it was known for two groups to observe a festival on a different day from each other. Did that happen on this occasion?

The Essenes regularly celebrated festivals on other days from the acknowledged religious authorities. Did the Essenes observe Passover at a different time that year and did Jesus follow an Essene practice in this matter?

Sometimes the Pharisees and Sadducees disagreed about a date. However, the main example was Pentecost, not Passover. Also, in such a case, the Sadducees often gave in to the mainstream practice of the Pharisees and the majority of the people. It saved trouble.

The most convincing explanation shows that there is no contradiction between John and the other gospels. When the priests refused to enter Pilate's premises in order to avoid a defilement which would have prevented them eating the Passover, John is not talking about the *seder* meal. Like Jesus, they had just eaten this the night before. He is referring to the *Hagigah*.

Numbers 28 and 29 list all the special sacrifices which were to be offered in the Temple for each different festival, Passover included. Each sacrifice was the *Hagigah* for that festi-

A special *seder* plate, containing the various items needed for the Passover meal.

val. The roasted egg, which is placed on the *seder* plate with the other symbolic foods, is a reminder to this day of the Passover *Hagigah*.

From almost every sacrifice that was offered, a portion was set aside for the priests to eat. The Passover that the priests still had to eat, and to which John was referring, was this same *Hagigah*. Nobody who knew the system would doubt otherwise.

If it was the evening *seder* which John meant, then there was no problem about ritual defilement. All the priests had to do was go through the *mikveh*, change their clothes and they would be clean at sunset. True, they could not have gone on duty in the Temple that afternoon for killing all the lambs, but there was no shortage of their colleagues for that task. All the priests and Levites, irrespective of what course they belonged to, served during

the festivals.

The *Hagigah* was a different matter entirely. The chief priests were due to deal with that only a few hours after they had sent Jesus to Pilate. It was the main sacrifice for the first day of the festival. As there was no way they could have removed ritual defilement before sunset, they had to stay away from Gentile contact. Nothing must debar them from the act of sacrificing and eating the Passover *Hagigah*.

Initial Preparations

Jesus sent Peter and John to look for a man carrying a jar of water who would show them where they would hold the evening *seder*. That in itself was unusual as it was strictly women's work to draw water. Amongst all the crowds in Jerusalem and all the women with their water jugs, that one man could not be missed.[5]

They then set about the preparations as Jesus had ordered them. Did this mean buying and preparing the provisions and setting the table? The most important thing was for the head of the household to sacrifice the Passover lamb. As group leader, that task fell to Jesus and he had no doubt performed it often in the past. Was he delegating it to Peter and John this time or were they looking after the other things whilst he dealt with the lamb?

Could we, perhaps, consider the possibility that there was no lamb on this occasion? Did Jesus present himself to his disciples as the Lamb of God who was shortly to offer himself on the cross as a redemptive sacrifice? They would not understand the implications of such symbolism at the time but it became clear afterwards. If this theory is correct, it makes Paul's later reference to Jesus as the Passover Lamb even more telling.[6]

Pilgrims often bought their animals from the flocks reared by the Temple authorities and sold for the sacrifices. Some scholars hold that the Bethlehem shepherds were looking after Temple sheep. If you brought your own animal, there was no guarantee that the examiners would pass it for use. It seems that they used to declare an animal unfit on the grounds of some blemish which its owner was not qualified to challenge, thus forcing him to buy from the Temple stocks.

The Temple also ran a money changing business as people had to exchange their ordinary money for the Temple coinage in order to buy an animal. Festivals were peak trading times and the money changers took advantage of their monopoly. Did Jesus and his disciples buy their lamb from the traders?

Killing the Lamb

The afternoon before the *seder* saw every available priest and Levite on duty. The heads of households brought their lambs to the Temple entrance where they were admitted in three groups. The gates opened, the first group surged in and, as the courtyard filled, the gates were closed.

To the accompaniment of a choir singing the *Hallel (*Psalms 113–118), each man led his lamb towards the altar. Flanking the altar stood two rows of priests, each holding a gold or silver bowl. In turn, every man stationed himself before a priest and killed his lamb by cutting its throat. The priest caught the blood in his basin then turned to the priest behind and poured the blood into his basin. The second priest emptied the blood out beside the altar.

When the first group had finished the second was admitted and then the third. One wonders how they coped in one afternoon with up to six hundred thousand men and animals. Procedures were efficient and speedy and everyone knew the routine. The rabbis tell us that no group went beyond the time it took for the choir to chant the Hallel psalms two and a half times. Also, the Temple complex was far larger than most people realise, as we show in a later chapter.

Meanwhile, the men hung the dead sheep on hooks set in the courtyard walls where they flayed and dismembered them. There were never enough hooks on these occasions so they improvised. One with the right arm and the other with the left, they grasped each other by the shoulder, flung a hook over their linked arms, affixed their two carcases in turn and dealt with them with their free hands.

Theologically, Passover is the great festival

A Jewish family celebrate Passover together at their home in Jerusalem.

of redemption. For Jewish people its significance lies in the deliverance of their ancestors from slavery in Egypt and their emergence as a nation. To them, therefore, redemption is a national rather than a spiritual concept.

Christians see the Passover lamb as a type of Jesus, the Lamb of God sacrificed for us.[6] His blood purchased our spiritual redemption and freed us from bondage to the slavery of sin.[7] Thereby we become a new people of God, committed to a transformed way of life.[8]

Pentecost, Weeks or *Shavuot*

Shavuot, meaning weeks, is the Hebrew name for this festival because it is separated from Passover by a period of seven weeks. Pentecost is the Greek name for the fiftieth day when it was celebrated. Together, Passover and Pentecost mark the start and end of the harvest season; roughly from April to June.

We have no record of Jesus visiting the Temple at Pentecost though he probably did. John mentions an unnamed feast which might have been *Shavuot* as easily as any other.[9] As the second of the Pilgrim Festivals, it was an important occasion but it lacked some of the appeal of Passover and Tabernacles because it only lasted for one day whereas they extended into seven.

Counting the *Omer* and the Firstfruits

On the second day of Passover, the priests marked the start of harvest by cutting the first sheaves of barley and waving them in the Temple as the firstfruits of the coming harvest.[10] The rabbis tell us that they actually prepared a barley loaf and waved it rather than a sheaf.

From this day the people counted seven full weeks. During this time they all were busy reaping the grain, first the barley then the later ripening wheat. The period was called the Counting of the *Omer* or sheaf. Each day was officially noted in the Temple while special *Omer* calendars and a liturgical formula now mark the days in the synagogue.

The fiftieth day was the Day of Pentecost. The careful measurement of time during the *Omer* counting gives point to the statement, 'When the day of Pentecost had fully come'.[11] At Pentecost, the priests offered two wheaten loaves to God as the firstfruits of the completed harvest.[12] The Mishnah describes how they reaped, milled and sifted the grain through twelve graded sieves to give the finest flour. Each loaf was approximately twelve inches wide, twenty long and four high.

The New Testament sees these two grain offerings as symbols of Jesus and his saving work. He arose from the dead at Passover on the same day that the priests were presenting the barley bread to God in the Temple. He is the firstfruits of the resurrection life which all who trust in him will experience, both spiritually as believers and physically beyond the grave.[13] On the day of Pentecost itself, thousands of pilgrims heard the apostles' message and three thousand of them immediately believed. They were the firstfruits of the Church, the firstfruits of a spiritual harvest of souls.[14]

People offered firstfruits from other crops besides grain. The Torah lists seven species of the land subject to the law of tithing and firstfruits; barley, wheat, grapes, figs, pomegranates, olives and honey, usually assumed to be date honey.[15]

None except the grain was ripe by *Shavuot* but, nevertheless, God's portion was already allocated. Farmers noted the first signs of fruit on each species and tied a piece of straw around the stem. These would be brought to the Temple later, either as money or dried. Meanwhile, there was the grain tithe to bring, not to be confused with firstfruits, and any love gift to say thank you for God's special blessings.

At Pentecost the Holy Spirit was given and the Church was born. Jewish pilgrims, mostly of the diaspora and speaking many different tongues, heard the message each in their own language. Three thousand believed and others soon followed.[16] Within days many had left for home, taking to every part of the known world the amazing story of the latest happenings in Jerusalem. Tradition tells of the countries the apostles later visited as witnesses. Did they find hearts open to their message because word of this unique Pentecost experience had already gone before them?

The rabbis also link *Shavuot* with the giving of the Torah on Sinai. From Exodus 19 they deduce that this happened on the sixth day of the third Jewish month, Sivan. The calculations are reasonable and fit in happily with Christian insights. In the Torah, the emergent nation of Israel received a ready made constitution on which to pattern its new way of life. The young church also needed guidance as it moved forward into untrodden paths. It received the Holy Spirit.

Tabernacles, Booths or *Succot*

Succot, the autumn harvest for the summer crops, marks the end of the agricultural year. It is the only feast which commands the people to rejoice before the Lord, waving palms, willows, goodly fruit and leafy branches.[17] The rabbis take the goodly fruit to be the *etrog*, a kind of large lemon. The leafy branch is the myrtle.

God also ordered them to build temporary shelters, or booths, and live in them during the festival week.[18] This reminded them that even in the security of their own land, they were just as dependent on God as they had been in the wilderness. Modern Jews still wave the so-called four species in the synagogue at *Succot* and build booths in their gardens.

Jesus spent at least one *Succot* in Jerusalem.[19] During the week he taught in the Temple. We have already seen how famous rabbis taught and led discussions on the Torah at the festivals for the benefit of visiting pilgrims. Here Jesus takes his place with them as a teacher. Once again, the scholars of the day marvelled at his learning seeing that he had 'never studied'.[20] As we have already shown, he may not have studied Torah under one of them but he was not uneducated or illiterate.

What did Jesus see as he looked around the Temple during *Succot*? The altar of sacrifice was decorated with willow branches. Processions of worshippers circuited the altar waving willow branches while choirs of Levites sang psalms to instrumental accompaniment. Much was made of the refrain 'Hoshana'.[21] We think of hosanna as a cry of praise. It was, in fact, a petition, 'O Lord, please save us'. On the final day, called the day of the Great Hosanna,

Notices in Jerusalem announcing distribution of straw for making booths for *Succot*.

the procession circled the altar seven times. John rightly referred to it as 'the last day of the feast, the great day'.[22]

Water and Light

The daily water libation ceremony was really an enacted prayer for rain seeing that the new agricultural cycle could not begin without it. Even in countries with ample rainfall, a relic of this ritual survives in the synagogue liturgy for *Succot* when a prayer for rain is recited.

The water libations reached a climax on the day of the Great Hosanna. Happy crowds surrounded the Temple hoping to see the high priest as, in a procession of song and instrument, he wound his way down the steep hillside to the pool of Siloam. There he filled a golden flagon of about two pints' capacity and carried the water back up to the Temple. In a symbolic gesture, he poured it out at the base of the great altar. Was it at that climactic moment that a voice cried out, 'If anyone thirst, let him come to me'?[23] Why not? Jesus was a great communicator. He chose his words and planned his timing with rare skill.

The Sadducees rejected the water and willow rituals because they had no basis in Scripture. They were only part of the Oral Law. Alexander Yannai, a Jewish king in the century before Jesus, was also the high priest and a Sadducee. Forced to perform the water libation in deference to the people, he showed his contempt for it by pouring the water on his feet. The angry crowd pelted him with their *etrogs*. He ordered in his soldiers and the rejoicing ended in massacre.

Four huge candelabra were erected in the Temple courts. They were so high that the younger priests climbed up ladders to replen-

Worshipper holding the four fruits used to celebrate *Succot*.

ish the oil and trim the wicks which were made from the worn out trousers and belts of the priests. When they were lit, even the darkest alley received light from them. Shortly after the festival Jesus claimed, 'I am the light of the world'. Did the glow of these great lights still fill the imagination, ensuring that the lesson was easily discerned?[24]

The Talmud describes how crowds gathered each evening in the floodlit courts to watch acrobats, dancers and jugglers. Rabbi Simeon ben Gamaliel, president of the Sanhedrin and leader of the Pharisees, used to juggle with eight flaming torches. The same man taught

Ex-Prime Minister Netenyahu lights the first *Hanukkah* candle.

Boy dressed in a priest's costume for the festival of Purim.

Paul and offered wise advice about the apostles.[25] Did Jesus ever see his juggling feats? Was he one of the Pharisees who argued with him or who voted for his death? One likes to think not.

Succot is the only feast with a Gentile dimension. On the first day thirteen bulls were sacrificed, twelve on the second day and so on in decreasing order. By day seven, seventy beasts had been slain.[26] The rabbis say that there are seventy Gentile nations in the world and each bull was an expiatory offering for one of them.

Zechariah 14 refers to the time when the Lord is king over all the earth and the nations gather annually in Jerusalem to keep the feast of Tabernacles. Appropriately, those who refuse to come are deprived of rain. *Succot* points to a Messianic rule of justice and peace in the world. Jewish people talk about living in the *succah*, or booth, of the world to come. Christians believe that Jesus is the Messiah and many link *Succot* with his second coming and millennial reign.

Dedication or *Hanukkah* and Other Feasts

There were other festivals. The day for the blowing of the ram's horn was two weeks before *Succot*. It is now the Jewish New Year.

The Day of Atonement was four days before *Succot*. *Purim*, associated with the story of Esther, was in early spring. Jesus surely observed them but we have no record of it and will not describe how they were kept.

John's gospel alludes to one other feast, the Dedication.[27] It was December and Jesus was walking with the disciples in the Temple in the shelter of Solomon's porchway. It rings true. Jerusalem is over three thousand feet above sea level. If it is wet or windy it is cold.

The Dedication, better known as *Hanukkah*, acknowledges events of 164 BCE. A foreign king oppressed the Jewish people and forbade them to practise their own religion. Many died as martyrs before the Maccabee freedom fighters entered Jerusalem and gained control. They at once threw out the images which desecrated the Temple and rededicated it.

When they came to light the seven branched, golden candlestick there was oil for only one day. The problem was that it took seven days to procure the special oil from Galilee and prepare it. Did they wait or light up with what they had? They chose the latter and the Talmud tells how the oil lasted for eight days until the new supply was ready. Whether one believes the story or not, there is no doubt that a common miracle in the Bible is the extension of some commodity in short supply.

Jewish people ever since have commemorated the miracle each December by kindling lights. They use nine branched candlesticks with candles for eight days and a 'servant' candle from which the others are lit. It is not a divinely ordained celebration but it does remind us of Jesus, the Light of the World, and how he traditionally arrived in the world at this same time of year, to be the servant of humankind.

Bible references

1	Deuteronomy 16:16, 17	9	John 5:1
2	Isaiah 62:10–12	10	Leviticus 23:10, 11
3	Matthew 23:27	11	Acts 2:1
4	John 18:28	12	Leviticus 23:15–17
5	Luke 22:7–13	13	1 Corinthians 15:20–23
6	1 Corinthians 5:7	14	Acts 2:5–13; James 1:18
7	1 Peter 1:18, 19	15	Deuteronomy 8:8
8	Ephesians 4:22–24	16	Acts 2:5–11, 41
		17	Leviticus 23:39–41
		18	Leviticus 23:42, 43

19 John 7:1–15
20 John 7:14
21 Psalm 118:25
22 John 7:37
23 John 7:37, 38
24 John 8:12
25 Acts 5:33–39; 22:3
26 Numbers 29:13–32
27 John 10:22

CHAPTER ELEVEN

The Temple Jesus Loved

Long before Solomon erected the first Temple, David had gathered the necessary materials, drawn up plans based on the Tabernacle layout and worked out a system for its day to day running.[1] Solomon gets the credit for what was truly a magnificent structure but he merely followed the blueprint already provided. Solomon's Temple was destroyed in 586 BCE by Nebuchadnezzar. When the exiles returned home, they built the second Temple (c.539–400 BCE). It was a much humbler affair but it endured.

In the years before the birth of Christ, Herod the Great tried to lift his stock with his Jewish subjects by virtually rebuilding the Temple. Although the overall design was the same, he created a lavish edifice, famed throughout the world. In spite of the rebuilding, it was still held to be the second Temple.

Herod took forty-three years and spent exorbitant sums on beautifying the Temple yet the rabbis never mention his beneficence. They loved their wonderful sanctuary but they hated Herod and all he stood for. It was always their way to block out the distasteful.

The manner of the Temple service originates from the book of Leviticus in the sacrifices and festivals ordained for the Tabernacle.

Over the centuries, specific ways of doing things evolved. By the time of Jesus they had become part of the Oral Torah and were as binding as the original biblical injunctions.

Priests, Levites and Laity

The Temple was controlled by the priests, aided by the Levites. For a fuller discussion about them, see the chapter on Groups Jesus Knew. Priests and Levites did not minister full time. Most of the year they lived in their own towns. Jericho, for instance, was known to be a town with a large population of priests. It is close enough to Jerusalem to have made an ideal base.

The priests were divided into twenty-four groups, each with a leader.[2] Luke tells us that Zechariah was in the eighth course of Abijah.[3] Each section had a week on duty twice a year while every priest served during the festivals. All the priests on duty from a given area met at a local centre then went up to Jerusalem together, allowing time for purification rites before starting their duties. The Levites also served by rota and travelled to Jerusalem with the priests.[4]

Before long, ordinary laymen also formed

themselves into parallel divisions and went to Jerusalem to support the priests. They gathered outside the Temple for the daily sacrifices and burning of incense. Laymen who could not go up prayed in their synagogues at home at these same times. They were called the *ma'amadot*, which means those who 'stood alongside' the priests. The priestly courses were known as the *mishmarot*, those who 'kept' or 'maintained' the Temple services.

As was said in an earlier chapter, Nazareth was a meeting place for the priests and Levites. Some of the Nazareth men must have been members of the *ma'amad*, doubtless from the selfsame synagogue that Jesus frequented. Was he, perhaps, a member himself? It would account for the fact that he seemed to visit Jerusalem for most of the major festivals, as the Gospels show.

An Old Story with a New Slant

Set against this background, certain aspects of the good Samaritan story become clearer.[5] We read that a certain man was going down from Jerusalem (3,000 feet above sea level) to Jericho (1,000 feet below sea level). Note that you always go up to or down from Jerusalem, irrespective of the compass direction from which you approach. It not only signifies the height of the city but also its spiritual elevation as the centre of Jewish religious life.

After robbers had left the man half dead, a priest travelling down the road saw him and passed by on the other side. The significant

Bird's eye view of an authentic scale model of Herod's Temple, showing the vast surrounding courtyards and central sanctuary building.

word is 'down'. Was he going home after his week in the Temple? Had he been going up, people would have exonerated his behaviour. By touching what might have been a corpse, he could have incurred seven days of ritual impurity and have been debarred from his duties. Going down, he had no excuse.

Likewise a Levite passed by. This suggests that he also was going down. Even if not, he had less excuse than the priest, for his tasks had less religious significance. Although it did not affect their work, the religious men put their own affairs above someone else's need. An enemy alien, whom no one expected to help, put them to shame.

The Appearance of the Temple

When we talk about the Temple, we usually mean not only the central shrine itself but the whole layout of courtyards and buildings which surrounded it. Our knowledge of what it all looked like comes from two main sources, Josephus and a tractate of the Mishnah called *Middot*. *Middot* means 'measurements' and this work describes the Temple size and layout. Josephus offers a more visual description of its splendour.

As with the feasts, the gospel writers had no need to describe the Temple. Most of their readers had either seen it for themselves or had at least heard about its grandeur for it was a well-known wonder of the ancient world.

The Court of the Gentiles

The area covered by the Temple complex was a levelled platform of some 1,000 feet square. Into this space would fit six maximum or eighteen minimum sized soccer pitches and, in both cases, still leave a 50 foot strip all round. No soccer field exceeds 450 by 300 feet or is less than 300 by 150 feet.

The main entrance was on the east, through Solomon's gate where Jesus walked at Hanukkah.[6] This magnificent porch is calculated to have been as long and as high as York Minster. Anyone, Jew or Gentile, could enter the outer courtyard, hence its name, the Court of the Gentiles. It covered an area about 750 feet square into which the squared measurement of four full sized soccer pitches would fit.

Here were assembled the money changers and traders whom Jesus challenged. Actually they did an important job, as we have already touched upon in the previous chapter. Jews and proselytes had to pay an annual, half shekel, Temple tax. They paid in either Galilean shekels or the coinage of the sanctuary. Shortly before a festival, money changers set up stalls all over the land to take the tax.

Here is the setting for the story of Peter and the fish with the coin in its mouth.[7] Visitors from abroad not only paid the half shekel Temple tax but needed their foreign currency changed. Therefore, the money changers conveniently traded in the Court of the Gentiles during festivals. As they held the monopoly, they made good profits.

There was also a market in the Temple for animals and meal and drink offerings. The rabbis record how exorbitant were the prices demanded, including the fee for examining an animal brought by a worshipper to determine its fitness for use. The Temple market seems to be what the rabbis call 'the Bazaars of the sons of Annas'.

Annas was a former high priest who still dominated affairs, including Caiaphas, his son-in-law, who was high priest at the trial of Jesus.[8] Josephus and the rabbis tell of the terrible greed and corruption of Annas and his family. People hated the way they cheated and took advantage of them. Once, the servants of Annas attacked and beat the crowd with sticks.

Such abuses explain why Jesus twice lashed out against the system and why the authorities concerned, knowing their unpopularity with the crowds and fearing repercussions, did not stop him.[9] Did it, in part, also account for the way the chief priests treated Jesus at his trial? They had a personal score to settle.

The Court of the Women

North of the Gentile enclave was a raised enclosure surrounded by a four foot high marble screen. Josephus says that Latin and Greek inscriptions forbade Gentiles to pass beyond this screen on pain of death. Archaeologists have since found two of these plaques. Paul uses the 'Wall of Partition', as the screen was called, to describe the barriers between Jews and Gentiles which are removed as the two peoples unite through faith in Jesus.[10]

Another superb porch, the Beautiful Gate, led into this courtyard. Here Peter and John cured the lame man soon after the Day of Pentecost.[11] This inner preserve was called the Court of the Women because Jewish women gathered there for any rituals which affected them. They were not allowed to go any further but they could look into the inner courtyards

The Courts of Israel and the Priests

Still more steps led through the Nicanor Gate into a comparatively narrow strip called the Court of Israel. Here only Jewish men entered. Cleansed lepers and women coming for purification after childbirth presented themselves before a priest at the Nicanor Gate but did not pass through.

Beyond the Court of Israel, and two steps higher, was the Court of the Priests. Taken together these two precincts measured 280 by 200 feet and were therefore larger than the Court of the Women.

Set into the surrounding walls were storage and work chambers for everything to do with the Temple service, including a place for animals due for sacrifice. There were stoves for the comfort of the priests, cooking, dining and sleeping quarters. An underground passage led away from the Temple to toilets and washrooms. There was also the hall where the Sanhedrin sat and other halls for official occasions.

In the Priests' court stood the fifteen foot high altar of burnt offering and the huge brass laver. A clever mechanical apparatus drew water from one of the many cisterns supplying the Temple and daily filled the laver. The cisterns were supplied with water carried by aqueduct from pools which are still there, some miles outside Jerusalem.

Much water was needed for ritual washings and generally keeping things wholesome. The Temple authorities had to be particular about hygiene in such a hot climate. Constant swillings of blood and refuse ran down into the Kedron valley through a complex drainage system. As a result, the valley was one of the most fertile spots in the country.

View through the Nicanor Gate of the doors of the Temple, Herod's Temple model.

from a raised platform. The Court of the Women was about 200 feet square.

Thirteen trumpet money boxes, already mentioned on page 104, stood against the walls of the surrounding walkway. Chambers in the corners of the court were used to store wood for the altar and oil and wine offerings. In others the nazirites cut their hair on completion of their vows and cleansed lepers made their ritual ablutions. The fact that a room was needed for lepers seems to show that leprosy was often a skin condition which eventually cleared up and was not always the disease we associate with that word.

The Central Shrine

The main feature of the innermost court, and indeed of the whole complex, was the Temple building itself. It was a long, narrow structure which appeared wider because of the rooms flanking it on either side. According to Josephus, its massive foundation stones were of marble overlaid with gold.

Like the Tabernacle, it comprised two sections. The outer was the Holy Place. Here the priests entered daily to burn incense and to trim the seven branched golden candlestick. Once a week they also changed the loaves on the table of shewbread. The inner sanctum was the Holy of Holies. The rabbis explain how a double curtain divided the Holy Place from the Holy of Holies. No one ever entered the inner shrine except the high priest, and that only once a year.

When the high priest went in on the Day of Atonement, he passed behind one end of the front curtain, walked between the two curtains and emerged into the Holy of Holies around the other end of the back one. This was the veil which tore in two when Jesus died.

If this part of the Temple needed repairs, they let workmen down through a hole in the roof in a basket which gave access to the walls while hiding the sanctuary from view. Not that there was anything to see! It should have contained the ark of the covenant covered by the mercy seat with its golden cherubs. That seems to have disappeared when the first Temple fell. The Roman general, Pompey, took Jerusalem in 63 BCE. He entered and found an empty room with a solitary block of stone.

The Temple at Work

The priests did far more than offer daily sacrifices, burn the incense, care for the lamps and provide the weekly shewbread. In addition, there were special sacrifices ordained for *Shabbat,* new moons and other festivals and fasts. They also dealt with the public.

Practically every aspect of a religious person's daily life focused on the Temple. The priests received freewill gifts, tithes, offerings and firstfruits. They absolved vows, supervised the rituals to do with the redemption of the firstborn, the conclusion of a nazirite vow or for a cleansed leper. These, and many other obligations enjoined in the Torah, all came under their province.

Ancient temples were fortresses. The Jerusalem one was no exception. When Nebuchadnezzar invaded the city it took him three weeks to reach and destroy the first Temple. Temple police and soldiers maintained order and security. When the chief priests began to fear that Jesus would cause them trouble with Rome, they sent their officers to arrest him during the feast of *Succot.* The men were so impressed by his teaching that they returned without him.[12]

Temples were also treasure houses. Apart from the wealth daily filling its trumpet boxes, the Temple treasures and furnishings were without price. No wonder they locked the gates and set a guard at night. So important was this evening routine that it was elevated to the status of being the last of the daily services. It was known as the *Ne'ilah* service, from a root meaning to lock up.

The closing service of the Day of Atonement today is also called the *Ne'ilah*, in memory of the custom. The name is doubly appropriate

Plan of Herod's Temple

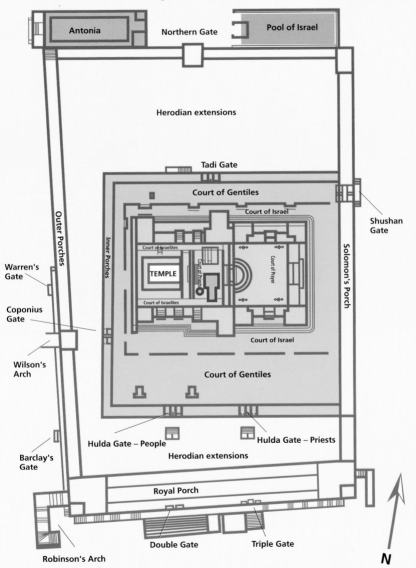

Antonia

Northern Gate

Pool of Israel

Herodian extensions

Tadi Gate

Court of Gentiles

Court of Israel

Shushan Gate

Warren's Gate

Inner Porches

Outer Porches

Court of Israelites

Court of Israelites

TEMPLE

Court of Priests

Court of Prayer

Solomon's Porch

Coponius Gate

Wilson's Arch

Court of Israel

Court of Gentiles

Barclay's Gate

Hulda Gate – People

Hulda Gate – Priests

Herodian extensions

Royal Porch

Double Gate

Triple Gate

Robinson's Arch

N

because of the metaphorical tradition that the gates of heaven are open for repentance during the ten days preceding *Yom Kippur*. Finally, as the day ends, so the gates of Heaven close and this special season for repentance is over.

Zechariah and the Incense[13]

The priests arose before dawn to prepare for the day's work. Firstly they processed in two companies around the precincts to see that all was well. While some got on with other tasks, those whose turn had come for special duty cast lots to determine the honours. The first lot decided who would prepare the altar; the second, who would offer the sacrifice; the third, who would burn the incense; the fourth, who would burn the sacrifice. The lots also applied to the evening, except for the incense when they cast again.

A priest might go a lifetime and not be chosen for certain duties. Once chosen for the incense, a man was not eligible for this duty again except in unusual circumstances. The incense lot was not cast with the others but only when certain preparations were completed.

The sound of the machinery pumping water into the laver alerted the *ma'amadot* assembling outside as to what stage proceedings had reached. A priest brought out the lamb for the sacrifice and prepared it. Then, with three trumpet blasts the porch gates were unlocked to admit the *ma'amadot* into the outer courts.

At the same signal, the officiating priest killed the lamb and sprinkled the altar. Other priests entered the Holy Place to trim the lamps and prepare the altar of incense. Finally, on the occasion we all know about, the incense lot was cast and fell on Zechariah. Carrying the incense, he entered the Holy Place alone. Outside, the priests and *ma'amadot* stood silently praying and waiting for him to emerge.

Although everyone wondered about Zechariah's experience, few would doubt its validity. Heavenly visions and voices were part of the religious tradition stretching back to the patriarchs. Visions were usually private appearances whereas the voice was heard publicly and was called a *bat kol*, literally daughter of a voice. The manifestation occurred three times during Jesus's ministry.[14] Some said that it was thunder but others recognised the words. Was the ability to understand dependent on a person's attitude towards Jesus and spiritual humility before God?

It is commonly taken that Zechariah and Elizabeth were old. Their age should be seen as relative to a woman's childbearing span rather than extremity of years. A priest who became old or who had an infirmity was relegated to humbler tasks. The fact that Zechariah was eligible for the incense lot implies a high standard of fitness. We do not know, but it is reasonable to conjecture, that he was in his later fifties. Elizabeth was probably in her early fifties, just beyond the menopause.

Liturgy and Music

Music, particularly the human voice, was immensely important in the Temple. Choirs of Levites sang in unison for all the daily services. Their words were taken from the Psalms, especially from those which are antiphonal. They sang the *Hallel* at all the big festivals. As it also concluded the family Passover *seder*, we know what psalms Jesus and the disciples sang before they left for the Garden of

A rabbi sounds the *shophar*, or ram's-horn trumpet, during a prayer service in the Patriarchs' tomb, Hebron.

Gethsemane.[15] At *Succot*, the Levites stood on the fifteen steps of the Nicanor Gate and sang the fifteen Psalms of Ascent.

The choirs performed with instrumental accompaniment. The rabbis list thirty-six musical instruments which were used, compared to the fifteen or so mentioned in the Bible. Chief were the lute, harp and reed pipe or flute. Cymbals marked certain parts of the liturgy.

The priests blew the ram's horn on fast days and for the autumn feast of Trumpets, now the Jewish new year. They also blew silver trumpets to announce the dawn of a new day and the opening of the Temple gates and to show the start of *Shabbat* at sunset. Archaeologists have found a carved stone referring to the place of the blowing of trumpets. They believe it once marked the part of the ramparts where the priest stood to blow so that all Jerusalem might hear the signal.

Naturally, the liturgy included prayer. The priests daily recited the Ten Commandments and the *Shema* with the short blessings that go with it. At certain times, the *ma'amadot* prostrated and chanted, 'O give thanks unto the Lord for He is good' or, 'Blessed be His name whose glorious kingdom is for ever and ever'. Whenever the priests pronounced the divine name, the people responded, 'Blessed be the Lord God, the God of Israel, to all eternity'. These refrains are still used in Jewish prayer today.

During the daily sacrifices certain priests ascended a platform and, hands outstretched, intoned the priestly blessing over the assembled crowd.[16] At certain places in the synagogue liturgy today, men who are traditionally of priestly descent still pronounce this same blessing over the congregation. There was also an eighteen part prayer which had become a regular part of the service by the time of Jesus. As so much of the Temple liturgy has come down to us through the synagogue, we deal with it more fully in a separate chapter on prayer.

Types of Heavenly Realities

Alfred Edersheim, a nineteenth-century Jewish scholar who believed in Jesus, felt that scenes of heavenly events in the book of Revelation were modelled on the ceremonial of the Temple. It could be so for John, the writer, must have been very familiar with its routines.

In view of the fact that much of the ceremonial was conceived by men, might it not be more correct to express this the other way round? By divine inspiration, scenes in the Temple were modelled on heavenly realities. It was very important that Moses carefully followed the pattern of the Tabernacle which God had given him. The book of Hebrews constantly tells us how the various rituals and institutions of the Tabernacle, and later the Temple, were types of truths within heaven itself.

Whichever way we look at it, the link is significant as even the few following examples show. For instance, there is a wonderful picture of a great crowd in heaven singing, 'Hallelujah', while the twenty-four elders prostrate themselves and worship God. A voice comes from the throne and the crowd answer in antiphonal response.[17] What a reminder this scene is of Temple choirs, ministering priests and the *ma'amadot* responding at each stage of the service.

The real significance of some passages in

Blowing the *shophar* at Jerusalem's Western Wall on the eve of a festival.

the book of Revelation can only be seen within the Temple context. It seems that if a Temple guard was found asleep at his post at night, his clothes were removed and burned as a punishment. Immediately, the following warning about watchfulness takes on a new urgency 'Blessed is he who is awake, keeping his garments, so that he will not walk around naked and be ashamed in public'.[18]

In one of the references to the glorified Jesus, he is standing beside the golden candlesticks and is wearing a golden girdle, not around his waist but across the breast.[19] Anyone familiar with Temple rituals would understand the implications. Here is a priest ministering in the Holy Place. Given the context, he is probably trimming the lamps.

Note that the girdle was more like a sash than a belt. Priests always wore their girdles across the breast. Moreover, they only put them on to perform their official duties and took them off when they had finished. The fact that, in this case, the girdle was golden suggests that we have a picture of the high priest himself. He was dressed in what were known as his golden vestments which he only wore on great ceremonial occasions.

When the priest on whom the lot fell went into the Holy Place to burn the incense, everyone withdrew from the inner court. All activity ceased in every part of the Temple. At a given signal, the officiating priest offered the incense and the worshippers outside fell down before Lord with hands outspread. There was a moment of total silence. Compare this scene with the description in the book of the Revelation when the seventh seal is opened. There is silence in heaven for half an hour. An angel with a golden censer offers incense on the golden altar which stood before the throne. The smoke rises, carrying aloft the prayers of the saints.[20]

Bible references

1 1 Chronicles 23–26, 28:11–21
2 1 Chronicles 24:1–19
3 Luke 1:5
4 1 Chronicles 25, 26
5 Luke 10:25–37
6 John 10:23
7 Matthew 17:24–27
8 John 18:13
9 John 2:13–16; Luke 19:45–48
10 Ephesians 2:14
11 Acts 3:1–10
12 John 7:32, 45–47
13 Luke 1:8–22
14 Mark 1:11, 9:7; John 12:28
15 Mark 14:26
16 Numbers 6:24–26
17 Revelation 19:1–9
18 Revelation 16:15 RSV
19 Revelation 1:13 RSV
20 Revelation 8:1–4

CHAPTER TWELVE

Prayers Jesus Prayed

Prayer was an important part of Jewish life. All the famous Bible characters prayed and some of their prayers are recorded and would have been known by Jesus. He must also have been familiar with the many Hebrew words linked with prayer in the Scriptures. Even a quick glance at some of them shows how, in themselves, they provide a theology of this great spiritual discipline.

Common are such terms as; call on God, cry out for redress, cry aloud for help, a ringing cry of joy or grief, seek God, seek God's face, inquire, ask, beseech, encounter, lift up, pour out, complain, expostulate, confess, meditate, recall, thank, praise, adore, worship, intercede, plead. The Psalms alone cover the whole emotional range of our relationship with God. It is surely their complete relevance to the human condition which makes them so greatly loved.

The prayers of the Bible are both spontaneous and liturgical. Contrast Abraham's plea for Sodom and Gomorrah with Solomon's dedication of the Temple. Jesus knew the value of both forms. He went into the hills to commune alone with God but he taught his disciples the liturgical formula which we know as the Lord's Prayer.

We can all think of stories Jesus told to teach important lessons about prayer. He wants us to pray in his name and according to the Holy Spirit's insight. He discourages pointless repetition and outward show. He encourages faith, humility, importunity and forgiveness. Most of these New Testament truths are, without doubt, also implicit in the great prayers of the Hebrew Bible.

It is wise not to read Christian insights into the prayers recorded in the Hebrew Scriptures. There, a plea such as, 'Lord save us', is more likely to be a request for deliverance from danger or oppression than for the salvation of the soul.

The same applies in the New Testament and the story of the Philippian jailer is a case in point. When he asked Paul, 'What must I do to be saved?' he was probably more concerned about his skin than his soul as he was accountable to the authorities for any disturbance in his prison.[1] Paul reassured him about the prisoners then astutely took advantage of the crisis to turn the issue into an evangelistic opportunity.

Jesus recited many liturgical prayers in the synagogue and on other religious occasions. They were in Hebrew, which is still the customary language of Jewish worship. Jewish people still say them today in their synagogues, albeit with some variations.

We cannot examine all the prayers which Jesus would have known. Many of them, perhaps modified somewhat, are still found in regular Jewish Prayer Books. These are easy to obtain and invariably provide translations into English along with helpful notes. Indeed, we can learn much about the meaning and mode of sincere prayer from the Jewish Prayer Book.

The Structure of Jewish Prayer

Almost all Jewish prayers are constructed from a basic unit called a benediction or a blessing, from its opening words: 'Blessed art Thou'. The blessing is a short statement of praise and thanksgiving to God. It acknowledges some benefit or duty springing from the relationship between God and humankind.

Grace before food is one of the oldest and simplest examples of a benefit received. 'Blessed art Thou, O Lord our God, King of the Universe, who bringest forth bread from the earth.' Jesus said grace when he fed both the five and the four thousand.[2] So did Paul when he encouraged everyone to eat and gave thanks, just before the shipwreck.[3]

We have already seen an example of a blessing linked to a religious duty in the chapter on education, where Mary lit the Sabbath candles. Two others are associated with putting on the prayer shawl and the phylacteries or *tephillin*. Both begin, 'Blessed art Thou, O Lord our God, King of the Universe, who hast hallowed us by His commandments'. For the prayer shawl it continues, 'and hast commanded us to enwrap ourselves in the fringed garment'.

For the *tephillin* it says, 'and hast given us command concerning the precept of the *tephillin*.' Jesus must have used them both.

The Pharisees who accused Jesus and his disciples of neglecting to wash their hands before eating were familiar with the words, 'Blessed art Thou, O Lord our God, King of the Universe, who hast sanctified us with His commandments and hast commanded us concerning the washing of the hands'.

At this juncture, it is appropriate to deal with three matters which arise from this commonly used form of wording. Firstly, a blessing sometimes cites a command, such as the washing of the hands, which is not found in the Written Torah. It is, however, part of the Oral Torah and that gives it binding authority in the Jewish community.

Secondly, such a blessing states that we are sanctified (made holy) by obeying God's commandments. This concept is laid down in chapters 17 to 20 of Leviticus. There we are presented with the constantly reiterated ideal, 'I am the Lord your God . . . therefore do this, don't do that . . . you must be holy as I am holy.'

These chapters show that holiness is not an abstract, stained glass and haloes kind of piety. It is obedience to God's laws and it is rooted in a practical outworking of one's faith. This is equally true in the New Testament as is clear from Jesus' teaching in John 14—16. If we love him we will obey his commandments. In that way, everyone knows that we are his disciples.

Thirdly, it may look as if there is a grammatical slip in the language used. In fact, the English translation correctly follows the Hebrew original. God is formally addressed in the second person singular, 'Blessed art Thou'. Then, as if the worshipper is overawed by the majesty of the creator king, he switches to the third person. He does not say, as we might expect, '(Thou) who hast sanctified us by Thy commands' but, '(He) who hast sanctified us by His commands'.

Judaism has a great sense of the holiness of God. This also explains why the English translations of Jewish prayers preserve the old fashioned dignity of 'thee' and 'thou'.

Of the numerous blessings known today, at least a hundred were used in Jesus' time and their composition was attributed to the Men of the Great Assembly. A century after Jesus, Rabbi Meir claimed that every Jew should recite a hundred blessings daily. On average, that means one every ten waking minutes. Some were said at home, some belonged to the synagogue liturgy while others, then as today, had an *ad hoc* function.

When you see a rainbow you praise God for the sign of his universal covenant. If you experience a natural phenomenon or freak of nature you proclaim God's wonders. After a safe journey or deliverance from danger you thank God for his mercies. For every occasion there is an appropriate response. Was it with this background in mind, though not necessarily in this manner, that Paul ordered Christians to, 'Pray without ceasing!'?[4]

Some blessings consist of one or two paragraphs rather than a sentence, such as the grace after meals. This is also found in the Passover liturgy and was no doubt one of the concluding prayers of the Last Supper. Jesus may not have followed the exact Hebrew words used today but the overall subject matter would have been similar.

It begins, 'Blessed art Thou, O Lord our God, King of the Universe, who feedest the whole world with Thy goodness.' A paragraph follows about God being the unfailing source of food for all creation. Next comes thanksgiving for redemption from Egypt, God's covenant with Israel, the sustaining properties of the Torah and the land of inheritance. As is the way of the longer blessing, it ends with a summary of the main points, 'Blessed art Thou, O Lord, for the land and for food'.

Another longer blessing is the *Havdalah* prayer which Jews recite at the close of Sabbath. *Havdalah* means separation; in this case between the holy Sabbath and the secular weekdays. Like the *Kiddush*, it is ascribed to the Men of the Great Assembly. It is too beautiful not to quote in its entirety. 'Blessed art Thou, O Lord our God, King of the Universe, who makest a distinction between holy and profane, between light and darkness, between Israel and the heathen nations, between the seventh day and the six working days. Blessed art Thou, O Lord, who makest a distinction between holy and profane.'

Most longer prayers came from the regular synagogue liturgy which was based on the Temple order of service. The longest Jewish prayers tend to be a composite series of separate but related blessings, each consisting of one short paragraph.

The best known is the *Amidah* or standing prayer. In Hebrew, *amidah* means standing and the congregation always stands for its

Wearing a prayer shawl, a Jewish man prays the morning prayers near a village outside Samaria.

recital. It is also called the Eighteen Benedictions for, although it now contains nineteen sections, eighteen was the original number. Alternatively, because it is one of the greatest and oldest Jewish prayers, it is simply designated, The Prayer, *HaTephilah* in Hebrew.

The *Shema*

The *Shema* is not really a prayer but, then as now, it was Judaism's great credal declaration of the unity of God. 'Hear, O Israel, the Lord is our God, the Lord is one'. Because of the Christian understanding of a triune Godhead, Jewish people interpret it today in anti-trinitarian terms. In the Mosaic age when it was first enunciated, and even at the time of Jesus, it was a lone affirmation of monotheism in a polytheistic world.

The schools of Hillel and Shammai debated when and how the *Shema* was to be said. They did not need to discuss whether it should be recited or not. The custom was already well accepted by their day. The scribe who tested Jesus' orthodoxy was amply satisfied when he answered by quoting its opening words.[5]

The Temple service opened with the *Shema*, so called from its opening words, '*Shema Yisrael*' or 'Hear, O Israel'. It quotes three paragraphs from Deuteronomy 6:4–9, 11:13–21 and Numbers 15:37–41. It may have been preceded by the Ten Commandments as the Nash Papyrus (2nd century BCE) shows that both were recited in the Temple. Whatever the case, the Ten Commandments are now no longer said regularly in the synagogue lest people forget that they are but a summary of the Torah and not its entirety.

A one paragraph blessing introduced the Shema, called the *Ahavah Rabbah* from its Hebrew opening. It starts, 'With great love have you loved us, O Lord our God, and great and overflowing tenderness have you shown us'. This moving prayer thanks God for giving Israel his teaching and asks that he will enable them to 'understand, discern, mark, learn, teach, heed, do and fulfil' all the Torah.

We cannot help but note and wonder about the similarity between these words and the second collect in Advent in the Book of Common Prayer. Referring to the Scriptures, it asks that we may, 'Hear them, read, mark, learn and inwardly digest them'. If any copying did take place, then it is the Jewish prayer which is the older one. The Jewish prayer ends, 'Blessed art Thou, O Lord, who hast chosen Thy people Israel in love'.

The *Shema* closes with another blessing, *Emet VeYatziv*. 'True and firm . . . is your word unto us for ever and ever.' It goes on to affirm God's enduring kingdom and faithfulness and the trustworthiness of his words to Israel for all generations.

It is doubtful if Jesus would have followed the exact wording in use today for either of these two blessings. What is certain is that their content was laid down long before his day. This is true of all the prayers we shall look at. The two other blessings associated with the *Shema* which appear in Jewish prayer books were added later.

The *Amidah*

The Temple service then moved on to the *Amidah*, the most important and best loved prayer in Judaism. Its eighteen short blessings are of great antiquity. A nineteenth paragraph was added at the end of the first century CE although it is now twelfth in the present order.

Even though Jesus never knew the additional benediction, we quote it because it does play a central part in the history of the separation of the church from the synagogue. 'And for slanderers let there be no hope, and let all wickedness perish as in a moment; let all thine enemies be speedily cut off, and the dominion of arrogance do thou uproot and crush; cast down and humble speedily in our days. Blessed art thou, O Lord, who breakest the enemies and humblest the arrogant.'

The reason for adding an extra benediction is as follows. The earliest people to follow Jesus were Jews. Even after the fall of Jerusalem in 70 CE, Jews who believed in Jesus continued to keep the Torah and worship in the synagogues. The rabbis did not necessarily know who were followers of Jesus but they always disliked them and sought ways of removing them from synagogue congregations.

It was the custom for everyone to stand and recite the *Amidah*. The rabbis introduced this new benediction but phrased it much more strongly than the form given above. It was clearly aimed at the Jewish believers. They could not publicly pronounce what was, in effect, a curse against themselves. If they stayed silent, they admitted to being part of the hated movement and were liable to be expelled. They could either deny Jesus or withdraw from the synagogue. Most did the latter.

The first three blessings of the *Amidah* are attributed to the Men of the Great Assembly in the fourth century BCE. They offer praises to the God of Israel's forefathers who sustains the living, keeps faith with the dead and whose name is holy for all generations. Part of the second blessing is as follows: 'Thou sustainest the living with loving kindness, revivest the dead with great mercy, supportest the falling, healest the sick, freest the bound, and keepest thy faith to them that sleep in the dust. Who is like unto thee, Lord of mighty acts?'

The middle twelve prayers are petitions. They were introduced in the period leading up to 70 CE, some perhaps during or barely before Jesus' lifetime. Can we envisage the disciples asking Jesus what he thought of those new benedictions which had recently been introduced into the *Amidah* and how the discussion might have developed until, eventually, they asked him to teach them how to pray? It may be fanciful but it is plausible too.

The twelve petitions begin with six requests for individual well-being. They first ask for spiritual benefits of insight, knowledge, repentance and forgiveness. Only then do they seek deliverance from oppression, healing for the sick and suffering and freedom from want. This last request is stated thus, 'Bless this year unto us, O Lord our God, together with every kind of the produce thereof, for our welfare; give a blessing upon the face of the earth. O satisfy us with thy goodness and bless our year like other good years. Blessed art thou, O Lord, who blessest the years'.

The next six petitions deal with matters of national well being. They talk about the restoration of Israel, the ingathering of her exiles, God's reign of righteousness, Israel's leaders and the righteous of the nation, the rebuilding of Jerusalem, the establishing of David's messianic throne and the raising up of his offspring to rule thereon and, finally, that prayer will be answered. What a rousing, messianic prayer for the ingathering of Israel's exiles this is! 'Sound the great horn for our freedom; raise the ensign to gather our exiles, and gather us from the four corners of the earth. Blessed art thou, O Lord, who gatherest the dispersed of thy people Israel.'

The three closing benedictions are thanksgivings from Maccabean times. They look for the restoration of the Temple and its services which had ceased during the persecution, thank God for his mercies and request peace for Israel. Here is the closing blessing. 'Grant peace, welfare, blessing, grace, loving kindness and mercy unto us ånd all Israel, thy people. Bless us, O our Father, even all of us together, with the light of thy countenance; for by the light of thy countenance, thou hast given us, O Lord our God, the Torah of life . . . and may it be good in thy sight to bless thy people Israel at all times and in every hour with thy peace. Blessed art thou, O Lord, who blessest thy people Israel with peace.'

Basically, the first and last three blessings of the *Amidah* always stay the same. The middle twelve are omitted at festivals and replaced by one or more alternative blessings appropriate to the occasion. For example, the intermediate blessing for the Sabbath speaks about, 'The tablets of stone on which was written the observance of the Sabbath'. God gave it to Israel to 'be satiated and delighted with Thy goodness seeing that Thou didst find pleasure in the seventh day and didst hallow it'. It closes 'Purify our hearts to serve Thee in truth . . . and may Israel, who sanctify Thy name, rest thereon. Blessed art Thou, O Lord, who hallowest the Sabbath.'

The Lord's Prayer[6]

Sadly, much Christian prayer today often seems to have lost touch with its Jewish and biblical roots. Too often it is self-centred and narrow. We are all guilty. Four important characteristics of biblical and later Jewish prayer highlight this fact.

Firstly, the priority is to magnify God's name and not to gratify personal wants. Secondly, even in petition the emphasis is on the community 'we' and rarely on the personal 'I'. Thirdly, there is a genuine spirituality expressed in desires for repentance, forgiveness and the ability to be worthy of God's mercies. Lastly, the requests for spiritual well being come before those for physical needs and outweigh them.

The Lord's Prayer is the great example of what prayer is about and the model for us to follow. It also typifies the best in Jewish prayer as is shown by the way it conforms to each of the points above. It opens with worship and adoration, it is couched in the first person plural, it seeks for numerous spiritual blessings and makes only one request for physical needs, namely our daily bread.

Were it possible to quote the whole *Amidah*, we would see how the Lord's Prayer aptly summarises its entire contents in a few, brief headings. This is not to say that Jesus modelled his words on the *Amidah*. He needed no one to teach him. It rather suggests that the compilers of the *Amidah* were men of godly insight who understood the true nature of prayer.

Space precludes a full study of the Lord's Prayer but we must mention a few things. To begin with, there are no incantations or invocations to mystic powers. This does not strike us, today, as being of great consequence, but any Gentile reader, coming from a polytheistic background, would immediately be impressed.

Moreover, Israel's God is the focus throughout, not as an abstract force but as a loving father. The repeated reference to him in Jewish prayers as 'King of the Universe' states the belief that he is the creator and sustainer of the world, but there are prayers to him as Father, especially in the Dead Sea Scrolls.

In choosing Israel as his covenant people through whom he would work out his purposes for the world, God was Israel's father in a very specific sense. He was also a father to anyone who was prepared to trust and serve him, as new Gentile believers in Jesus were very soon to find out.

Jesus often called God 'my father'. This was a messianic claim. The rabbis deduce from Scriptures about God having a son that the Messiah would be so close to him that only he would have the right to call God 'my father'.[7] At the same time, they never understood this in the sense that the virgin birth implies.

We then pray that God's name be made holy. Is it not intrinsically so by his very nature and not subject to change? Judaism has a concept of the sanctification and the profanation of The Name. God's people can bring his name into disrepute by unseemly behaviour. We ask that we will not do this but rather, will honour his name in the world by our mode of life. This will happen when he is sovereign of our lives and we try to put his will before our own desires. In this way we help to bring the rule and ways of his kingdom into the world.

A *codex* found among the Dead Sea Scrolls. There are many prayers to God as Father in the Dead Sea Scrolls.

In requesting our daily bread, the Greek uses an obscure word which puts the emphasis, not on our regular, constant need for provision, but simply on what is required for the moment. Tomorrow's needs are tomorrow's concerns, not today's.

Forgiveness of our sins is made dependent on our forgiving those who have in some way sinned against us. The rabbis taught that a sacrifice in the Temple was of no effect if the person who brought it had not repented. Jesus went further. He said that even if our conscience is clear but we realise that someone else bears us a grudge, we must try to sort things out before our sacrifice will be acceptable.[8] This does not negate the principle of forgiveness by grace. It does speak of the need to maintain right relationships with other people.

In all these things we need help to resist Satan, the Evil One, who would bring us down. We cannot overcome the power of evil in our own strength. Judaism teaches about the evil and good inclinations which we all possess. They are of equal strength and, in theory, it should be as easy to overcome the one as to allow the other to predominate.

This is not so in the light of Scripture or personal experience. It is not what Jesus teaches here. Christianity holds the doctrine of original sin. We battle against Satan and our fallen nature. Only God's power can help us to overcome such forces and for this we must pray.

The closing paean of praise does not appear in every version and is considered to be a later addition. Be this so or not, it accords perfectly with the sentiments of worship and adulation which have characterised Jewish prayer from its earliest days. The words form a fitting conclusion to a model prayer.

Bible references

1	Acts 16:25–34	6	Matthew 6:9–13
2	Matthew 14:19; 15:36		Luke 11:1–4
3	Acts 27:33–35	7	2 Samuel 7:12–16
4	1 Thessalonians 5:17		Psalm 2:7; Proverbs 30:4
5	Mark 12:28–30	8	Matthew 5:23, 24

CHAPTER THIRTEEN

The Synagogue Jesus Attended

The synagogue is Judaism's most stable and beloved institution. By the time of Jesus it was already a well-established and important focus of religious life for Jewish people everywhere. This is clear from the New Testament as well as other sources. There, synagogues are mentioned sixty-seven times and forty-three of these occasions are connected with Jesus. Indeed, had it not been for the popularity of the system, Judaism might not have survived after the destruction of the Second Temple and the loss of all that went with it.

This third-century synagogue stands over the synagogue that Jesus knew in Caperrnaum.

Origins

Before dealing with that issue we must first examine how the synagogue originated. No one knows exactly when synagogues began but scholars feel it was during the Babylonian exile in the 6th century BCE. The word comes from the Greek and means a place where people gather together. This seems very appropriate. With their Temple in ruins and their homeland made desolate and barred to them, it is easy to see how the Jewish exiles might have gathered together in each other's homes for mutual support.

Before long, it became the custom to meet officially on Sabbaths and festivals. As they recalled the Temple services, the exiles might then have initiated the custom of reading the relevant Torah portion for the occasion. Soon, the meetings would take on a structure and leaders would emerge. Later they might acquire a building as a meeting place and centre for community affairs. In short, the synagogue was born.

We assume that the exiles who returned home brought the system back with them along with a rudimentary standard service of Torah readings and prayers. We certainly know that the elders who succeeded Ezra and Nehemiah were a worshipping community who fasted, read the Torah, made confession and prayed together.[1] They, and those who followed them, are called the Men of the Great Synagogue or the Great Assembly. From them sprang the Sanhedrin, the nation's great governing body and chief court of religious law.

The men of the Great Assembly were responsible for setting Judaism on the course that it has followed ever since. They helped to develop the Oral Torah. We note elsewhere how they wrote prayers and established liturgical procedures which were familiar to Jesus and which are part of Jewish worship throughout the world even at this present time.

The earliest known synagogue was in Alexandria where a slab was found dedicating the building to Ptolemy III (246–221 BCE). The inscription implies that the institution was already by then a stable feature of Jewish social and religious life. The rabbis record that by 70 CE there were three hundred and ninety-four (some say four hundred and eighty) synagogues in Jerusalem alone, including one within the Temple precincts.

Numerous archaeological remains have been found all over the Mediterranean region and the known world of that time. Clearly, synagogues existed wherever there were Jews. This fact is endorsed in the book of Acts. Few tourists visit Israel without a trip to the ruined synagogue in Capernaum. It is typical of other such sites and from them we can deduce what the buildings were like.

Layout

Most ruins indicate an edifice similar in area to a medium sized church. The design, usually of a main hall divided lengthways into three parts by two rows of columns, shows the influence of Greek basilica architecture. Buildings always face Jerusalem from whichever location they are in. They often had an upper storey but this does not imply that women were separated from the men up there. Some scholars believe that there was segregation but we do not know.

At the end of the building orientated

towards Jerusalem was the ark, a cupboard containing the scrolls of Scripture. A controversy between Hillel and Shammai describes how it was covered with embroidered curtains sewn with little bells. The congregation used benches facing the ark while the elders sat on ornate chairs with the ark behind them. These were the best seats which the scribes liked to occupy to signal their importance in the community.[2]

A wooden platform, the *bimah*, stood in the centre of the hall. It was modelled on the raised platform in the Temple where the priests stood to bless the people. The congregation sat around the *bimah* on the three sides where the worshippers could see the ark. Upon the *bimah* was the reading desk from where services were conducted. We gather that there were lamps as the Mishnah tells of the oil used to keep lights burning throughout the whole day of Atonement.

Synagogue layout remains much the same today, be the building as large and ornate as a cathedral or merely a simple structure with a sanded floor. Only in modern times has Progressive Judaism done away with the

Cutaway illustration of the synagogue at Capernaum, showing the adjoining cloister, the women's gallery and the tabernacle where the Torah scrolls were stored.

bimah and turned attention to a platform at the front, more in the style of a modern, Protestant church.

Progressive forms of Judaism have also streamlined and modernised the services. Certain prayers are shortened or omitted. The Torah is often read in English. Women and men sit together. Women's voices and instrumental music are used in the choirs while women cantors and rabbis are becoming common.

Ancient synagogues were smaller and simpler than today, the most notable exception being in Alexandria. The synagogue there apparently provided seventy-one gilded chairs for members of its great council. It was said to be so big that many people could not hear the reader and an official signalled when to make the appropriate responses.

In Gentile areas, synagogues were often located outside a city near water. Sometimes this was because there was no room or the authorities did not allow them to be built within the city. Also, the Jewish community often preferred to worship as far away as possible from a heathen place which, as Philo explained, was tainted with idolatry. In addition, somewhere near running water made it easier to perform any ritual ablutions.

When Paul was in Philippi one Sabbath, he went outside the city gate to the river where he assumed he would find a place of prayer. He was not looking for an open air meeting, as we usually imagine, but for a proper building.[3]

Officials and Their Duties

Each synagogue had its elders, often men of substance, who were experts in both the Written and Oral Torah. They formed the local sanhedrin or religious law court. It was to such men that the centurion appealed when he asked them to petition Jesus for the healing of his servant.[4]

The elders chose a president from their number as the ruler of the synagogue. The ruler arranged the services and chose people to lead the prayers, read the Scriptures and give the sermon. He had the prerogative of inviting visitors to address the congregation, as happened with Paul on many occasions.[5]

One such dignitary challenged Jesus for

Ark containing the Torah scrolls from a synagogue in the Old City of Jerusalem.

Remains of the Hurva synagogue, Jerusalem.

healing a woman who was bent double on the Sabbath.[6] Jesus raised to life the daughter of another ruler, Jairus.[7] Crispus, the leader of the Corinth synagogue, became a believer.[8]

A *hazzan* or minister had charge of the property and running of the services. He took the scrolls from the ark for readers and replaced them at the end. He was the attendant who gave the book to Jesus and received it back again in the synagogue in Nazareth.[9] He might well be a scribe and, in a small place, the schoolmaster too.

As the sun set, the *hazzan* announced the start of Sabbaths and festivals with three trumpet blasts from the synagogue roof. The first warned that Sabbath was imminent and gave a brief opportunity for people to finish their activities or do a last minute task. The second indicated that housewives should light

the Sabbath lights and say the blessing. From that moment, work must cease. The third proclaimed that Sabbath had begun.

A less happy duty for the *hazzan* was to administer the punishment of scourging which took place in the synagogue.[10] Jesus warned his disciples that they would be scourged in the synagogues for following him.[11] Paul tells us that he was scourged five times.[12]

As few people completely understood the public reading of the Hebrew Scriptures, a translator stood by the reader to translate into Aramaic. He proceeded verse by verse for the Torah and every three verses for the Prophets. Sometimes this was another of the *hazzan's* duties.

The custom first evolved in the exile. A young generation of Jews soon grew up who spoke Aramaic and were no longer fluent in Hebrew while later generations had even more difficulty in understanding it. The translation, or *targum*, was not precise but rather a free rendering which might well undertake to explain or comment on a passage.

Such seems to have been the case when Ezra read the Law and the Levites stood beside him and translated the sense for the people.[13] Existing translations (*targumim*) date only from the third and fourth centuries CE. Nonetheless, they are valuable aids to understanding the Scriptures because they are based on earlier sources.

The Regular Services

Two of the three daily synagogue services corresponded to the daily sacrifices in the Temple. *Shaharit*, the dawn service, coincided with the daily morning sacrifice and *Minhah*, towards dusk, with the late afternoon offering.[14] *Ma'ariv*, after nightfall, simply acknowledged the time when Temple business shut down.

A *minyan* or quorum of ten men was essential for public worship. The reason for the *minyan* is deduced from at least three texts. Abraham pleaded with God to save Sodom if even only ten just men were found there.[15] Moses sent twelve spies to view the land of Canaan but the ten who gave a bad report influenced the whole community.[16] Boaz took ten elders of the city to witness his purchase of land from Naomi and marriage to Ruth.[17]

The Talmud accordingly infers from all this that ten males over the age of thirteen constitute a community or a congregation. Contrast the significance of Jesus' assurance that if only two people agree about a matter, the Father will respond, and that where two or three gather in his name, he is with them.[18]

If you travel by El Al or in an Israeli train, you often see a group of orthodox men gathering at the back of the plane or carriage at the time for prayer. Look out for someone going around and tapping likely looking travellers on the shoulder to persuade them to join and make up the required *minyan*.

Superimposed upon the daily rites, in the Temple and therefore also the synagogue, was the *Musaf* or additional service. Chapters 28 and 29 of Numbers detail specific sacrifices for all special occasions. These are Sabbaths, new moons which mark the beginning of the months, Passover, Pentecost, Trumpets or Jewish new year, Day of Atonement and Tabernacles. The system worked as follows.

Each Saturday, which was the seventh day of the week, the Sabbath sacrifice was offered in addition to the daily ones. If it happened to be the first day of the month, a new moon sacrifice was added. In this way the *Musaf* offerings for each festival were always made along with the daily ones. Similarly, the *Musaf* service in the synagogue always acknowledged the current festival celebrations in the Temple with appropriate readings and prayers. The synagogue liturgy still follows this pattern today.

Vocal and instrumental music played a notable role in the Temple but the latter had no place in the synagogue. Indeed, the music of the Temple is now forgotten. The rabbis banned it after 70 CE because it was too sad a reminder of all they had lost. Vocal music did become a synagogue tradition which has developed diversely down the centuries but we do not know to what extent it was used in the time of Jesus.

A few musicians feel that some indigenous churches in the Middle East, whose roots go back to the early church, might still preserve elements of Temple musicology in their ancient liturgies. How to determine them, if they are there, is almost impossible.

Structure of a Service

From the rabbinic sources we know how a traditional Sabbath morning service in a synagogue was arranged. Weekday meetings were similar but briefer as there was no time for extras or for a leisurely approach.

Some time in advance, the synagogue ruler selected the men who would take part in leading the worship. The first of these was the prayer leader. He opened proceedings by reciting the three paragraphs of the *Shema*, 'Hear, O Israel'. He also intoned the two blessings which accompanied the *Shema* and which are still used today. Then he led the worshippers in saying the eighteen benedictions of the *Amidah*.

After the prayers, a second person read the Torah portion fixed for the day. In the diaspora they followed an annual cycle, in the land of Israel, a triennial one. On Sabbaths, seven readers now take part but this is a later development. So, too, are the blessings with which the readers introduce and conclude the portion.

Public Torah reading on a Shabbat goes back at least to Ezra's time. Philo and Josephus call it an ancient practice and the New Testament corroborates this.[19] It was also read on market days, that is, on Mondays and Thursdays. People who left home too early to go to their own synagogue, assuming they had one, reached the market town in time for the service there. The synagogue leaders made a special effort to cater for the visitors and that included reading the Torah. Even in the western world, it is still read today on Mondays and Thursdays.

The prayer leader then returned to the desk, as it was his duty to read the passage from the Prophets. Whether this was fixed or chosen at random we do not know. The words used in the Nazareth story about Jesus finding the place are ambiguous.

Some say that the habit of reading the prophets dates back to the persecutions of the second century BCE when Torah reading was banned and the Prophets were substituted. Even when the decree was repealed, the custom continued. The New Testament twice mentions the practice. The first time is in connection with Jesus in Nazareth[20] and the second with Paul on his travels.[21]

Everyone looked forward to the sermon which then followed. Sometimes it was given by the prayer leader, as in the case of Jesus at Nazareth, or by some visitor or suitably qualified person. According to Philo, 'People flocked to the synagogue to hear a refreshing discourse from the best qualified who instructed them in things conducive to their welfare and general improvement'. Not surprisingly, a later rabbinic maxim states, 'Hasten to the synagogue eagerly and return slowly'.

The congregants also enjoyed any resultant discussion which was an accepted part of proceedings. It explains why wherever Paul went, his first evangelistic strategy was to visit the synagogue where he knew they would ask him to address the congregation.[22] He was not the first to use this method. Jesus did so before him when he travelled all over Galilee teaching and preaching in the local synagogues.[23]

A Service in Nazareth

When Jesus returned to Nazareth he went, on the Sabbath day, back to the synagogue which he and his family had always attended. As a local member who had become a celebrity, he was asked to lead the prayers and preach.[24] Imagine the scene!

On the *bimah*, surrounded by the worshippers and facing the ark, stood the prayer leader. We know it was Jesus because the same person always read the Prophets later. When he had recited the *Shema* and the *Amidah*, he stood aside while the attendant handed the Torah scroll, already open at the right place, to the person chosen to read the Torah. Jesus then returned to read the prophets. Afterwards, he gave the book back to the attendant and sat down, as the custom was, to preach. Luke outlines the routine very accurately.

There is really no problem about the portion of the reading quoted which comes from two places.[25] These were simply the verses which Jesus picked out as his text. This also accounts for the fact that he apparently stopped reading in the middle of a sentence. It was, and is, an acceptable device to take a text from part of a sentence or to link together two phrases from different chapters. As the whole passage had to be at least twenty-one verses long, Luke naturally does not quote it in full. He merely gives a marker as to what it was about.

At first, the subsequent discourse met with such absolute approval that one wonders what went wrong. Is the key in the words, 'Is not this Joseph's son?' rather than in any implied messianic claim which Jesus made for himself?

Did someone throw out a snide remark about the local carpenter with his simple, working class background, who was now making such pretentious claims?[26] Did someone else add a derogatory comment about his parents and brothers and sisters; just ordinary folks, all well known to the assembled crowd? Suddenly, in the laudatory discussion that followed, people were diverted from the wonder of Jesus' words to the pettiness of personalities.

Perhaps a sympathetic family friend then suggested that if Jesus would do a miracle for them, it would help to prove that his messianic claims had validity, despite his homely, local origins. He refused. Would it really have made any difference? Instead he told them that they were no better than the Gentiles and used stories about Elijah and Elisha to prove it.

This was the supreme insult. Was Jesus now sinking to their level in the discussion? No! Remember that he knew them; who was slow to pay for work done; who had cheated his father in some transaction; who was mean, quarrelsome, unkind. The implications behind his accusation were justifiably felt. They were furious and would have killed him if they could. If this reading of the story is correct, then, in the end, the question of his messiahship was very incidental.

The beautiful Abuhav Synagogue, dating from the 1490s, in the holy city of Safed, northern Israel.

The Synagogue and the Survival of Judaism

In 70 CE the Second Temple was destroyed and was never rebuilt. Many of the Jewish leaders, as well as ordinary people, died in the war. Some fled to countries of the diaspora and others went into slavery.

The Temple, with its sacrifices, priesthood and lavish ceremonial, was like a magnificent crown which displayed the wonder of Judaism to all the world. Remove the crown and what is left? What remained was surely a sad spectacle of disarray. Yet a king can survive without his crown provided the heart stays strong to pump the blood along the veins; and the heart and lifeblood of the Jewish people held intact. The Torah, Written and Oral, was the lifeblood which flowed through every stratum of Jewish society. The synagogue was the institutional heart of that society which linked and held its diversified elements together.

After 70 CE, those rabbis who remained regrouped and assumed the role of religious leadership. They set their common mind to answering the pressing religious questions that the loss of the Temple posed. Chief amongst them was the issue of atonement for sin.

If atonement for sin was made by sacrifice, how could it be atoned for now there was no sacrifice? The Hebrew word, *avodah*, in this context meaning service, referred to the Temple and its sacrifices. A Bible verse says, 'Serve Him with all your heart'.[27] 'What,' asked the rabbis, 'is the service (*avodah*) of the heart?' They answer that it is prayer. Prayer, then, becomes the substitute for sacrifice and the means of atonement. The synagogue was already the place for communal prayer. It now

Remains of the synagogue at Chorazin that Jesus might have known.

replaced and took over this function from the Temple.

We cannot go into details about how these rabbis worked or what they accomplished. Suffice to say that they transferred many Temple customs to the synagogue, if not in their entirety then at least in part. They introduced such things as the blowing of the ram's horn at the Jewish new year and the waving of the four species of the *lulav* (*etrog*, palm, myrtle and willow) at Tabernacles.

Though simple in themselves, these and many other things provided links with the old way of life and eased the severity of the loss. The synagogue and love of Torah kept Judaism alive at a time when it was in danger of dying out. Ever since, Torah observance and the Synagogue have continued to vitalise Jewish people dispersed all over the world and have preserved them, if not as a unified race, then as a religious entity.

Bible references

1 Nehemiah 9 & 10
2 Mark 12:38–40
3 Acts 16:13
4 Luke 7:2–5
5 Acts 13:15
6 Luke 13:14
7 Mark 5:22
8 Acts 18:8
9 Luke 4:17, 20
10 Acts 22:19
11 Matthew 10:17
12 2 Corinthians 11:24
13 Nehemiah 7 & 8
14 Numbers 28:3, 4
15 Genesis 18:32
16 Numbers 13
17 Ruth 4:2
18 Matthew 18:19, 20
19 Acts 15:21
20 Luke 4:17
21 Acts 13:15
22 Acts 13:14–16, 14:1, 17:1, 2
23 Matthew 4:23
24 Luke 4:16–30
25 Isaiah 58:6; 61:1–2
26 Mark 6:3
27 Deuteronomy 10:12

CHAPTER FOURTEEN

The Scriptures Jesus Read

Christians so glibly claim the Bible as their own particular book that they are surprised to learn that for Jewish people, the Bible is only the Old Testament. Even the terms Old and New Testament reflect a Christian theological bias which Jewish people find slighting. They do not feel that God's covenant with them has either been discarded or replaced. Their Scriptures have not been superseded by a record of superior things. Christians must accept that the New Testament neither excludes nor contradicts the teaching of the Old. Both are complementary and, indeed, incomplete without one another.

The Tanakh

Jewish people call their Scriptures the *Tanakh*, which is an acronym for three words; *Torah* (Law), *Neviim* (Prophets) and *Ketuvim* (Writings). This threefold division of the holy writings, which Christians call the Old Testament, was already known in Jesus' day. The books are the same but their order differs.

The oldest section was the Pentateuch or Torah, which consists of the first five books of the Bible. Traditionally authored by Moses, it records the instructions which God gave to Israel whereby they were to regulate their daily lives. These instructions were not given in a vacuum and, therefore, the Pentateuch describes the whole historical framework within which the Torah functioned.

Archaeology shows how, long before Moses, every ruler had scribes who recorded the business of his realm. A wise leader like Moses would surely have established a system of registering great national events. He must also have ensured that a record of the origins of the new nation under his care was kept. If nomadic Israel could carry the Tabernacle around, it could doubtless also have transported a growing accumulation of written material, be it on clay tablets or papyrus leaves.

We know that important codes of laws have been found, such as the Code of Hammurabi who was contemporary with Abraham. That Israel should have preserved its own code is no surprise. If the sources from which the Torah was compiled were gathered and preserved under the initiative of Moses then, in that sense, he is their author, irrespective of who edited them or when.

The second section is the *Neviim* or

Part of the Dead Sea Scrolls from the Shrine of the Book in the Israel Museum, Jerusalem.

Prophets. It is divided into the former and latter prophets which accounts for the different order of the Jewish *Tanakh* and the Christian Old Testament. The former prophets are Joshua, Judges, Samuel and Kings. They outline Israel's history from the settlement of Canaan to the exile. The latter prophets are Isaiah, Jeremiah, Ezekiel and the twelve small books from Hosea to Malachi. They summarise the teaching of all the great national prophets other than Daniel. He is classed with the Writings.

During this period historical records abounded. Joshua and Samuel documented important happenings.[1] Each king of Israel and Judah had recorders who duly catalogued the history of the realm.[2] Writings were known which no longer exist such as the book of the Wars of the Lord[3] and the book of Jasher.[4] Even in the anarchical period of the Judges some accounts of events must have been kept,

however imprecisely.

Rabbinic tradition ascribes the authorship of the book of Joshua to Joshua and of Judges and 1 Samuel to Samuel. Even though events are mentioned in 1 Samuel which took place after his death, the story is mostly about Samuel. Other items were probably assembled in his generation.

Regarding the latter prophets, did these men precis their own message in writing, as Jeremiah did when he dictated to Baruch or did their enthusiastic followers do it for them?[5] Either way, we assume that their contents are an accurate summary of their teaching. It is interesting that the Dead Sea scroll of Isaiah, which is dated to about 100 BCE and which is preserved in the Shrine of the Book in Jerusalem, offers a reading which does not significantly diverge from the present text.

Apparently, a scribal class came into prominence during the exile who spent time copying

The Tanakh or Hebrew Bible

TORAH (Law or Instruction)	Genesis	Exodus	Leviticus	Numbers	Deuteronomy
NEVIIM (Prophets)	**FORMER PROPHETS** Joshua	Judges	1 Samuel	2 Samuel	1 Kings
	LATTER PROPHETS Isaiah	Jeremiah	Ezekiel		
	THE TWELVE:				
	Hosea Nahum	Joel Habbakuk	Amos Zephaniah	Obadiah Haggai	Jonah Zechariah
KETUVIM (Writings)	Psalms Ecclesiastes	Proverbs Esther	Job Daniel	Song of Songs Ezra	Ruth Nehemiah

and editing the old documents. Nehemiah is said to have founded a library and collected material about the prophets and kings and the writings of David.[6] In all this literary activity, much of what had long been seen as holy Scripture received its present, familiar stamp. Ben Sirach for instance, writing around 180 BCE, refers to the twelve prophets, which dates them in that form to well before his day.[7]

The *Ketuvim* or Writings contain poetical and wisdom literature, mostly composed later than the Prophets. Books like Ruth, Chronicles (placed last in the *Tanakh*), Daniel, Ezra, Nehemiah and Esther, appeared too late for inclusion amongst either the former or latter prophets where they best fit.

Ecclesiastes and the Song of Songs were not easily accepted as being scriptural. Hillel, for instance, recognised Ecclesiastes and Shammai rejected it. Others, such as Job, Psalms, Proverbs and Lamentations, consisted of human outpouring and observation rather than the story of God's initiative in human affairs. They were therefore felt to be of inferior standing. In the end, because they were akin to the prophets in their spiritual impact, they were soon viewed as inspired.

The Law and Prophets were read regularly in public worship in Jesus' day, as we have elsewhere noted. The writings, being of a later

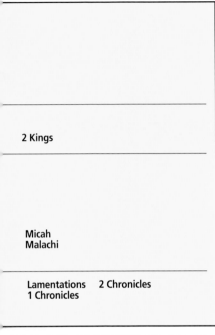

2 Kings	
Micah Malachi	
Lamentations 1 Chronicles	2 Chronicles

Yavneh, or Jamnia, site of the council that set the Jewish canon of Scriptures.

The 'jot' and 'tittle' of Hebrew script.

date, had not been around long enough to achieve this status although they were known. Jesus and Paul both quote from them when they talk about doing good to your enemies and heaping coals of fire upon their heads.[8]

This, incidentally, is not a sign of retribution but of blessing. In an age without matches, lighting a fire was hard and people did not let their fires go out. If they did, they borrowed live coals from someone else's fire to rekindle their own. They carried them, as they did most things, in a container on their heads. A single, glowing ember might die before it could be used. A good heap lasted long enough to achieve its purpose and ensure a good blaze for light, cooking and winter warmth. It spoke of comfort and generosity.

Closing the Canon

During the mid-second century BCE persecution under Antiochus Epiphanes, attempts were made to destroy the Jewish Scriptures. The contents of the Law and Prophets were already established but hard circumstances now forced the people to determine which of the Writings should be deemed canonical. Hence, by the time of Jesus, three categories of books were accepted as holy. Despite disagreement about the status of some of them, their number and content were as we know them today.

The prologue to ben Sirach's Ecclesiasticus (not to be confused with Ecclesiastes) was written about 132 BCE by his grandson. It mentions the Law and Prophets and other books. The other books were the Writings which were, with but a few exceptions, by then accepted as part of the canon as we now know it.

Josephus also recognised the same divisions and contents of the Jewish Scriptures. The New Testament talks about the Law and the Prophets. Luke's allusion to the Law, Prophets and Psalms could just be taken in the wider context of the Writings, for Psalms is the opening book of the *Ketuvim*.[9]

After the destruction of the Temple in 70 CE, certain rabbis emerged who helped Judaism to adjust to the new situation. Their base was a town called Yavneh or Jamnia, located just inland and a little south of modern Tel Aviv. Amongst the many matters they dealt with was the still unsettled question of the canonicity of Ecclesiastes and the Song of Songs. At the Council of Jamnia (*c*.100 CE) they finally ruled that they were scriptural.

The books were written separately on skin or papyrus rolls. At first, the exact words and letters of the text were not sacrosanct but Philo, Josephus and others all imply that by their time, the text was divine and immutable down to the letter. Jesus seems to agree when he says that no dot or iota will pass away from the Law.[10]

The Greek *iota* stands for *yod*, the smallest letter of the Hebrew alphabet. The dot is the tiny, decorative tag that is a feature of the Hebrew script. The omission or addition of a *yod* can make a big difference in meaning. The presence or absence of the decorative tag has nothing but an aesthetic value.

However enduring Jesus held the law to be, his outlook was not restrictive like that of many around him. Time and again he showed that compassion for suffering was more important than mere rules and regulations. He could thus enunciate the paradoxical principle that the Sabbath was made for man, not man for the Sabbath.

Perhaps it is Paul, Peter and the writer of the book of Hebrews who best summarise the New Testament understanding of the divine inspiration of the Scriptures. Not only do they acknowledge their source, they look beyond to their purpose in helping the believer to live a profitable, spiritual life.[11]

The Septuagint (LXX)

King Ptolemy Philadelphus of Alexandria (285—247 BCE) had a library of the best books in the world. When told that five were missing, his librarian, Demetrius, advised him to approach Eleazar, the high priest in Jerusalem. Tradition tells how Eleazar provided seventy scholars to translate the Torah into Greek.

Working simultaneously but separately, they produced identical translations.

Somewhere behind the legend lie the origins of the *Septuagint*, the translation of all three parts of the Hebrew Bible into Greek. The Greek word *septuagint* refers to seventy. So too, in Latin, does its commonly used abbreviation, LXX.

Here was the answer of Greek speaking, diaspora Jews to the same problem which produced the Aramaic Targumim of Palestine. However inviolable the Hebrew original, it was better to translate it into a language that people understood than to lose knowledge of it entirely or for it to become solely the province of scholars. Jewish Scriptures are still read publicly in Hebrew but they have, ever since, also been translated into the languages of every country where Jewish people live.

As the Jewish homeland was part of the Greek speaking world, the Septuagint was popular there too. In the early church it was particularly important for Gentile converts, all of whom would speak Greek, whatever their native tongue. Discipled by the Jewish followers of Jesus, they were taught the Jewish Scriptures, that is, the Tanakh, for there was no New Testament in those days. Their text book was the Septuagint.

Of course, it was not long before people began to write down the important parts of the story of Jesus' life. Paul wrote letters to churches which he had founded in order to help them in their understanding of their new faith. Others, too, wrote letters and recorded events that were happening around them.

Of all the documents which were produced in the apostolic age and however valuable they were to the growing church, they were not seen to be canonical at that stage. The same feeling could not immediately exist for the new writings that there was for the *Tanakh* which had been held sacred for so long. Only with the passage of time and the influx of a Gentile majority into the church did the idea develop that a second group of inspired writings might exist alongside the older body.

Although by the latter part of the 2nd century CE we see most of the books of the New Testament holding the place and authority that they do today, various individuals and sections of the church still differed slightly over which books they accepted. Not until the canon of Athanasius (367 CE) do we find a list which is exactly the same as our present New Testament.

We can understand, therefore, why the Septuagint was so important to the first Christians. It gave them a version of the Scriptures that they could read for themselves. Evidence of its widespread acceptance is seen in the way that subsequent New Testament writers used it. They quote about three hundred times from the *Tanakh*, and usually from the Septuagint translation. This is why many quotations do not completely tally with the Old Testament version that we are familiar with.

As time went by, so many Gentiles joined the new movement that the number of Jewish believers became a small minority. As a result, the Septuagint was perceived to be more of a Gentile, Christian tool than a Jewish one. The rabbis preferred to make their own, alternative translations rather than use it.

The Apocrypha

The Septuagint contains a number of books which are not found in the *Tanakh* and which are called the Apocrypha. They are Judith, Tobit, 1 & 2 Maccabees, Wisdom, Ecclesiasticus or the Wisdom of Sirach, Baruch and some material supplementary to Esther and Daniel. It also includes 3 & 4 Maccabees and four books of Esdras which are not traditionally part of the Apocrypha.

The Jerusalem canon rejected the Apocrypha but did accord it a certain measure of authority. The Alexandrian canon, still followed by some parts of the Church, accepted it as deutero-canonical. This means that it was inspired in the same way as the other books while yet being of secondary importance to them.

We only have to read some of the Apocrypha to understand this view. Daniel, for instance, contains the song of the three men cast into the fiery furnace which stands happily alongside any Psalm. The additional story of Daniel unmasking the trickery of the priests of Bel is scarcely more difficult to believe than that of the lions' den.

There are beautiful passages in Wisdom and Ecclesiasticus despite the wordy style which contrasts so heavily with the crispness of Proverbs and brevity of Ecclesiastes. The historical information in the books of the Maccabees, Baruch and Judith is most valuable. For instance, Judith describes events undocumented elsewhere and Baruch, probably written in the second or first centuries BCE, gives important information about Jewish diaspora communities.

At the same time a work like Tobit, with its supernatural themes of angels, demons, exorcisms and miraculous cures, hardly offers much of spiritual value. Others, like Judith and Susannah's story in Daniel, contain unedifying details of lust and violence; though such matters are equally to be found in books like Judges or Kings.

Some readers hold that the literary style of the Apocrypha does not compare with other biblical books, being mostly too verbose. Whatever the case, we can reasonably imagine Mary and Joseph gathering their growing family together on a Sabbath afternoon and recounting some of these stirring stories in a form suitable for young ears.

Two books are particularly interesting. Wisdom, probably composed by an Alexandrian Jew during the last century BCE, treats many themes found in the Bible. Wisdom 2 speaks of the brief span of human life in phrases reminiscent of Job. Chapters 10—12 recapitulate Israel's story as do some of the Psalms. Chapter 13 describes the futility of the hand carved idol in the same imagery as Isaiah 40:18–26.

Ecclesiasticus is sometimes known as the Wisdom of Jesus ben Sirach. It was written on the eve of the Maccabean revolt by one of the *Hasidim*. The author encourages devotion to the Torah and is eager to teach wisdom to all who crave it. In style it is similar to Proverbs, which is not surprising as they both belong to the same stream of wisdom literature.

Anyone interested in these matters can easily obtain a copy of the Apocrypha. The study edition of the Jerusalem Bible, with its extensive notes, not only contains the Apocrypha but draws greatly from the Septuagint for its translation. It is a helpful tool for use with this chapter.

Reading the Torah using a silver pointer at a Jerusalem synagogue.

Although there are no direct New Testament quotations from the Apocrypha, scholars note many affinities between the two which suggest that New Testament writers were familiar with it. To illustrate, compare the following phrases and thoughts from Wisdom and Ecclesiasticus with related New Testament passages.

Contrast: John 14:15 with Wisdom 6:18, 'Loving her (wisdom) means keeping her laws'; Romans 9:21 with Wisdom 15:7, 'Take a potter . . . out of the same clay, . . . he models vessels intended for clean purposes and the contrary sort, all alike; but which of these two uses each will have is for the potter

himself to decide'; 2 Corinthians 5:1–4 with Wisdom 9:15, 'For a perishable body presses down the soul, and this tent of clay weighs down the teeming mind'; Colossians 1:15 with Wisdom 7:25, 'She (wisdom) is a breath of the power of God, pure emanation of the glory of the Almighty'; Hebrews 1:3 with Wisdom 7:26, 'She is a reflection of the eternal light, untarnished mirror of God's active power, image of his goodness'.

Contrast: Mark 10:37 and Luke 14:8 with Ecclesiasticus 7:4, 'Do not ask the Lord for the highest place, or the king for a seat of honour'; James 1:13–14 with Ecclesiasticus 15:11, 'Do not say, "The Lord was responsible for my sinning," for he is never the cause of what he hates'; James 1:19 with Ecclesiasticus 5:11, 'Be quick to listen and deliberate in giving an answer'; James 4:7 with Ecclesiasticus 7:1, 'Shun wrong and it will avoid you'.

Pseudepigraphical Literature

Other writings, many dating from the first and second centuries BCE, were familiar to the people of the New Testament. The authors are not known because it was then the accepted custom to attribute a work to a famous, ancient personality. This is why scholars use the designation pseudepigraphical. It implies that the named authorship is not genuine. Thus, the full title for the book of Wisdom in the Apocrypha is the Wisdom of Solomon, although it was written long after Solomon's time.

There are books of Esdras (Ezra) and Enoch and Psalms of Solomon. A book of Jubilees purports to tell the world's history from Creation to Sinai. It provides much imaginative information such as the names of Adam's children after Cain, Abel and Seth and about the fallen angels. Note, however, that some of the so-called imaginative details may be drawn from ancient traditional sources. We do not know and we cannot distinguish between the two.

One special literary style was that of the apocalyptic. Such a work offers revelations about the unknown future and the end of the world. It uses fantastic imagery to symbolise coming cosmic cataclysms. The main purpose was to show how God will eventually punish evil and reward good by bringing the present world order to a climactic close. He will then inaugurate his own kingdom where the righteous will share with him in a reign of justice and peace. The book of Enoch is an apocalyptic work. We are familiar with the same genre in parts of Daniel and the Revelation of the New Testament.

The New Testament occasionally cites as Scripture a text which is not from the Old Testament at all but probably comes from one of these popular works. Because they treated of biblical subjects, they were held to have some measure of authority.

Jesus quoted a Scripture which said that rivers of living water would flow from the heart of those who believed in him.[12] Paul referred to a verse about the heart of man being unable to conceive what God has planned for those who love him.[13] Neither passage comes from the Old Testament. The latter might be from a composition entitled the Apocalypse of Elijah. Even the scholars are not always sure of the sources and some references obviously come from topical works which have since been lost.

Further allusions to matters not known from other Scriptures are how the famine in Elijah's day lasted for three and a half years;[14] the mysterious role of the angels in the giving of the Law;[15] and the spiritual rock which accompanied the Children of Israel in the wilderness.[16] Jewish tradition claims that the rock struck by Moses followed them thereafter and provided water for as long they needed it. We learn the names of the Egyptian magicians, Jannes and Jambres, who opposed Moses;[17] the ways in which some of the Old Testament martyrs died;[18] and how Lot deplored the evil of the people amongst whom he lived.[19]

Jude is very interesting in this respect. When he tells us about a controversy between the archangel Michael and Satan over Moses' body, he is probably quoting from a work called The Assumption of Moses. When he compares the false teachers of his day to 'shooting stars bound for an eternity of black darkness', he had the Book of Enoch in mind. There, stars stand for angels, in this case, fallen angels. He then mentions a prophecy about the end of the world and coming judgement which was attributed to Enoch, the seventh patriarch from Adam.[20]

There are some puzzling statements in Stephen's martyrdom speech which may refer to a lost tradition about Moses.[21] We read that Moses knew all the wisdom of Egypt and was a powerful man of word and action. When he was forty he visited his fellow countrymen and killed an Egyptian who was ill treating one of them. The question is, why did he visit his countrymen?

It goes on to say, 'He thought his brothers realised that through him God would liberate them, but they did not.' Then he tried to medi-

A young Jewish boy reads the Hebrew Bible.

matter and wanted to kill him.[22] Why should the slaying of some seemingly insignificant Egyptian official warrant Pharaoh's intervention and a man like Moses having to escape for his life? Remember that he had been reared in the royal palace and probably knew the reigning Pharaoh well. There may have been another reason.

There are certain extra-biblical traditions about Moses which we should neither accept indiscriminately nor reject outright. They tell us that his Egyptian name was Osarsiph and that he was educated in all the learning of his age. He became a popular and influential general who led a successful campaign against Ethiopia and married Tharbes, the daughter of the conquered king.

Did Moses, at the height of his military success and popularity, decide to lead his people in a revolt against their servitude? If so, he obviously failed. But an attempted rebellion by a provenly able well-liked general would indubitably have incurred Pharaoh's extreme anger. It would certainly explain these passages in Stephen's speech.

The Apocrypha and Pseudepigraphical writings show more than anything else how certain ideas were opening up within Judaism. One such was the existence and person of Satan. Another was the notion of spiritual death in contrast to physical death. This led to the concomitant distinctions between the resurrection of the body and the soul and to theories of reward and punishment beyond the grave. Even the doctrines of the Word and the Trinity are traced from this period. These concepts were to become some of the building blocks for Christianity which New Testament writers would adopt and adapt.

ate in a local quarrel and was asked, 'Who appointed you to be our leader and judge?' This is a strange question considering that it was another forty years before God called Moses to save Israel. The last verse of this passage is even stranger. When Moses did return to free Israel it says, 'It was the same Moses that they had disowned when they said, "Who appointed you to be our leader and judge?"'

From the Exodus narrative we learn that Moses fled for his life after he had murdered the Egyptian because Pharaoh heard of the

Bible references

1 Joshua 18:9; 24:26
   1 Samuel 10:25
2 2 Samuel 20:24, 25
   1 Kings 11:41; 14:19, 29
   et al
3 Numbers 21:14
4 Joshua 10:13;
   2 Samuel 1:18
5 Jeremiah 36:4
6 2 Maccabees 2:13–15
7 Ecclesiasticus 49:12

8 Proverbs 25:21, 22
   Matthew 5:44
   Romans 12:20
9 Matthew 22:40
   Luke 24:44
10 Matthew 5:17–19
11 2 Timothy 3:16, 17
   Hebrews 4:12
   2 Peter 1:20, 21
12 John 7:38
13 1 Corinthians 2:9

14 Luke 4:25; James 5:17
15 Acts 7:53
   Galatians 3:19
   Hebrews 2:2
16 1 Corinthians 10:4
17 2 Timothy 3:8
18 Hebrews 11:37
19 2 Peter 2:7
20 Jude 9,13–15
21 Acts 7:22, 25, 27, 29–35
22 Exodus 2:15

CHAPTER FIFTEEN

The Opposition Jesus Faced

Many people failed to understand Jesus or were unwilling to accept the things he taught and the claims he made. In this connection the New Testament has much to say about three of the most influential groups of the day; the scribes, the Pharisees and the Sadducees.

If we had only the New Testament record to guide us, we might be excused for feeling that these people were all bad. Not so! We must remember that the New Testament specifically picks out those instances where Jesus faced their opposition. Fortunately, we know enough about them from other sources to realise that there is another side to the story. If a group has its villains, it also has its saints and most people stand somewhere between the two extremes.

Pharisees and Sadducees

Historical Origins

As the origins of the Pharisees and Sadducees are closely linked, we shall look at them together. They first appeared as distinct parties in the 2nd century BCE but the trends from which they developed go back much earlier.

When Nehemiah opposed intermarriage between the returnee exiles and surrounding foreigners, he found that a small aristocracy of wealthy, Jewish families was implicated, including relatives of the high priest. It was another group, the religious purists of the day, who supported him. These extremes of attitude were reflected in the later philosophies of the Sadducees and Pharisees respectively.

After a silent period in Jewish history, Alexander the Great conquered Persia (334 BCE). His successors unified the peoples under their rule by hellenisation, the imposition of Greek religion and culture upon them. Many Jews resisted, choosing martyrdom rather than sacrifice to idols, profane the Sabbath or give up circumcision and their Torah. Those who withstood were ordinary, country folk, encouraged by certain religious devotees called the Hasidim or pious ones.

In Jerusalem, the wealthy nobility and the chief priests accepted hellenisation for both political and personal expediency. The following cases illustrate. A certain Jason bribed the Syrian rulers to let him build a gymnasium in Jerusalem for Greek games. Its profits accrued to him. A Joseph ben Tobias similarly bought the lucrative right to collect taxes in Judaea.

Here again were the two social strata from which our two groups emerged.

Religious persecution was at its height when a country priest and his seven sons formed a guerilla band of freedom fighters. The most famous son, certainly for Christians, was Judas Maccabaeus, because of Handel's oratorio. Thousands of Hasidim and ordinary people joined them. Before long they were fighting open battles and soon recovered occupied Jerusalem. They then rededicated the Temple which the enemy had desecrated (165 BCE).

From the Maccabee brothers arose a new ruling dynasty, the Hasmoneans. Initially the Hasidim and religious idealists supported the Hasmoneans but when later rulers succumbed to the influences of wealth and power, they turned against them. Indeed, the former champions of religious purism soon became part of that wealthy aristocracy whose ruling dictates were political expediency and self interest. At this time, too, the titles Pharisee and Sadducee emerged to describe the adherents of these two sections of society.

What's in a Name?

The Hasidim called themselves 'the pious ones' because they stood for the uncompromised purity of Judaism. They repudiated all Gentile ways and interpreted their religion so strictly that other people nicknamed them 'Separatists' or Perushim from the Hebrew *parush*; hence Pharisees.

The derivation of Sadducee is less certain. They may have had family links with Zadok, Solomon's high priest, thereby giving the term Zadokim or Zadokites. When anglicised, this translates into Sadducee.

A later theory is probably incorrect, simply because it was so late. Antigonus of Socho, a 3rd century BCE sage said, 'Be not like slaves who serve the master hoping for a reward but be as slaves who serve with no hope of reward.' One of his followers, another Zadok, took this to mean that there were no rewards in the world to come because there was no world to come. He also rejected the Oral Torah in favour of the Written Torah alone. According to this theory, the Sadducees took their name and beliefs from him.

Another idea is that they called themselves Zadokim or 'righteous ones' in response to the name Hasidim or 'pious ones'. Linguists question how the form Zadokim became Zadukim. One possibility is that the -u form represents some unknown peculiarity of dialect pronunciation.

A further suggestion is that, just as the nickname separatist or Pharisee took on, so a similar thing happened with the Sadducees. Some unsympathetic wag might have said, 'What, call themselves righteous? They almost destroyed everything with their compromising ways (from *zadu*, 'they destroyed'). They should be called Zadukim, not Zadokim!'

Under the Hasmoneans and After

The Hasmonean rulers grew in power, ironically, because they now made compromise agreements with the nations around them. The offices of king and high priest were united in the current ruler as a matter of course though the Hasmoneans had no natural right to either position. In spirit and action they grew closer to the Sadducees.

The Pharisees tolerated this provided they were free to live according to their own principles. Not surprisingly, when they did challenge

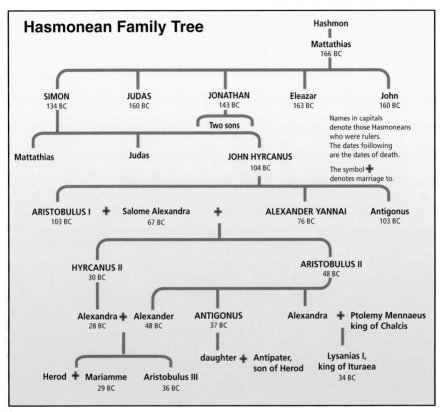

Hasmonean Family Tree

Hashmon

Mattathias
166 BC

SIMON 134 BC	**JUDAS** 160 BC	**JONATHAN** 143 BC	Eleazar 163 BC	**John** 160 BC

Two sons

Names in capitals denote those Hasmoneans who were rulers.
The dates foillowing are the dates of death.

The symbol ✚ denotes marriage to.

Mattathias   Judas   **JOHN HYRCANUS**
104 BC

ARISTOBULUS I 103 BC ✚ Salome Alexandra 67 BC ✚ **ALEXANDER YANNAI** 76 BC   Antigonus 103 BC

HYRCANUS II 30 BC   **ARISTOBULUS II** 48 BC

Alexandra 28 BC ✚ Alexander 48 BC   **ANTIGONUS** 37 BC   Alexandra ✚ Ptolemy Mennaeus king of Chalcis

daughter ✚ Antipater, son of Herod   Lysanias I, king of Ituraea 34 BC

Herod ✚ Mariamme 29 BC   Aristobulus III 36 BC

the policies of John Hyrcanus (135–105 BCE), son of one of the seven Maccabee brothers, he stated a preference for the Sadducees.

His son, Alexander Yannai (104–76 BCE), crucified eight hundred Pharisees who opposed him. Later he regretted this and advised his wife, who succeeded him, to be led by them. During her rule they held political power for the only time in their history. She also gave them seats in the Sanhedrin which

had been a Sadducee preserve up to then. When she died, her sons quarrelled over the succession until the Roman general, Pompey, took Jerusalem.

In 37 BCE Rome confirmed a convert to Judaism as king; Herod the Great. The Hasmonean dynasty was finished although Herod did marry into the family. He curtailed the power of the Sadducees by killing many and placing his own appointees in the

Sanhedrin. Those who remained were pragmatists and, because they joined forces with the newcomers, the party survived. Towards the Pharisees Herod was better disposed as he recognised their influence upon the masses.

After Herod, the country was divided and ruled by his sons who were answerable to Rome. The exception was Judaea where Roman procurators governed but left internal affairs in the hands of the Sanhedrin. The Sadducees, as one would expect, kept in with Rome and got as much out of the situation for themselves as they could.

By this time, the sincere religious piety of the Pharisees had lost its edge. Their early zeal had, generally speaking, been channelled into a stereotyped system of actions and responses. Nevertheless, because many individual Pharisees were sincere, the group as a whole had the support of the ordinary people. Also, both equally hated Rome.

The Pharisees still retained seats on the Sanhedrin and well knew how to manipulate the Sadducees and exert political power when it suited them. This was the situation in Jesus' day. It presents an interesting angle on his trial and the reasons for the crucifixion.

Ideologies of the Pharisees and Sadducees

For the Pharisees, the ultimate authority was the Oral Torah. So many of the precepts had been formulated by the Pharisees themselves, that we can easily see why they too often took precedence over the Written Torah. When Jesus accused them of leaving God's command in favour of men's traditions,[1] his words are confirmed by later rabbis.

Rabbi Johanan said, 'The scribes' words are . . . more believed than the words of Torah.

Torah contains both light and weighty precepts (i.e. binding to a lesser or greater degree) but the words of the scribes are all weighty.' Another saying was, 'It is a greater crime to teach contrary to the scribes than contrary to the Torah itself.' As the Pharisees and scribes both held the same attitudes towards the Oral Torah, it is applicable to use these quotations here.

The Sadducees rejected the Oral Law and took the Written Torah as their only authority. Naturally, they built up their own traditions but, in religion as in politics, expediency ruled. So, because the Pharisees had more influence over the people, the Sadducees gave in to their customs rather than create an outcry. For instance, the date of Pentecost was always fixed according to Pharisaic calculations and not the Sadducean way.

As is often the case in life, things are rarely a clear cut black or white. The fundamental issue for the Sadducees was probably not so much the validity of the Oral Law as the extent to which it was binding. For the purist Pharisees, this was categorical. For the pragmatic Sadducees, everything was negotiable.

Regarding ritual defilement and purification, the Sadducees ridiculed the obsessive extremes of the Pharisees. When Jesus ate in the home of a Pharisee, did he perhaps purposely not wash his hands in order to make an opportunity to teach him the basic principle of inner holiness?[2]

Surprisingly, the Pharisees were more lenient in some matters than their opponents because they adeptly found loopholes in the Torah and mitigating circumstances. For example, the Sadducees took the *lex talionis* (eye for eye, tooth for tooth) literally whereas

Part of a Hasmonean period coffin discovered during archaeological excavations outside Modiin, Israel.

the Pharisees were prepared to accept money in lieu of punishment.

Another example is that of levirate marriage. The Pharisees ensured the perpetuation of a man's name by advocating marriage to a brother-in-law only if the couple had been married and the husband had died before the woman had borne children. The Sadducees imposed it even if they had only been betrothed.

The Pharisees believed in the immortality of the soul and resurrection of the body to reward or punishment. The Sadducees denied resurrection and reward and punishment after death. They did not necessarily believe in annihilation and probably accepted the concept of a shadowy existence in Sheol. They may even have been merely agnostic, simply arguing that there was no proof in the Torah for such beliefs.

When Paul went on trial before the Sanhedrin he knew his accusers well.

Accordingly, he used this controversy between the Pharisees and Sadducees to create an internal argument between the two parties. He thereby diverted attention from other matters and created some sympathy for himself.[3]

When the Sadducees asked Jesus about the woman who had had levirate marriage with seven brothers, they were testing him on two issues; his attitude towards their interpretation of levirate marriage and his views about the resurrection. He bluntly told them that that they did not know the Scriptures from which they drew their authority and that there was no such institution as marriage in the resurrection. He then offered them a proof for resurrection from the Torah itself which they obviously did not accept.[4]

By New Testament times Judaism had developed an imaginative hierarchy of angels and demons. The Pharisees treated these schemes cautiously but wholeheartedly believed in the miraculous and the supernatural. The materialistic, this-worldly Sadducees felt uncomfortable with such phenomena and denied the existence of angels and demons.

Had the two factions been discussing the subject before they came jointly to Jesus to ask him for a sign from heaven?[5] Jesus was curt with them, then afterwards warned his disciples against the leaven of both parties. By this he meant their attitudes which were so much at variance with their teaching. The Pharisees looked for a supernatural sign but had no intention of accepting its implications. The Sadducees rejected the world of spiritual phenomena, even when they saw it evidenced and were offered proof from their own accepted authority, the written Torah.

Both groups struggled with the age-old problem of free will versus determinism. The Pharisees emphasised God's pre-ordination of affairs while yet recognising the influence of the human element of choice. Everything was predestined and both good and evil were instrumental in ensuring that what was purposed would come to pass. The Sadducees believed in man's free will and could not accept that God would fore-ordain anything evil.

The messianic expectations of the Pharisees looked for God's universal rule on earth. This would not come by political means but through God's divine power being vested in a human descendant of David. The Messiah would rule in peace and justice and all nations would submit to the yoke of Torah as interpreted by the Oral Law. The government would be in the hands of the righteous, namely the Pharisees themselves. No doubt the scribes, too, were included.

These beliefs all contributed to their antipathy towards Jesus. Should he prove to be the Messiah, what place could they expect to command in his kingdom? He was so critical of their behaviour. Further, what kind of a kingdom would it be under one who held their traditions in such low esteem?

The Sadducees had little time for messianic matters but they did worry lest Jesus antagonise Rome.[6] With their interest in the manipulation of political power, they surely envied Jesus his popularity with the masses. Furthermore, they misunderstood his teaching about the kingdom and feared where it might lead. Twice we read that the chief priests (and we must not forget that they were Sadducees) brought him to trial because of envy.[7] Those with a financial interest in the trading in the Temple also bore him a grudge for the two occasions when he threw the traders out.

No wonder these two parties, usually so antagonistic, made common cause against Jesus. Wherever we read about the chief priests (who were Sadducees) and the Pharisees joining together against him, we can be sure that the attitudes we have just discussed were the main motives behind their opposition.[8]

The Haverim

Evidence suggests that there were two types of Pharisee. There was an exclusive, extremely strict sect, numbering a few thousand, called the Haverim. This means an association of friends. The others, who were the majority, were also strict but were never as extreme as the Haverim.

In this connection it is interesting to speculate about which category Paul belonged to. He was trained under Gamaliel, a rabbi respected by religious Jews to this day. With his all or nothing zeal, might not Paul have been a Haver?[9]

When he defended his case before King Agrippa, Paul claimed that according to the most exact sect of his religion he had lived a Pharisee (Acts 26:5). This does not conclusively prove that he was a Haver, but certainly suggests the likelihood.

A Haver took vows concentrating on three topics; ritual purity, tithes and offerings and Sabbath observance. That these are the subjects on which Jesus and the Pharisees most often took issue, suggests that it was possibly the Haverim who were his main opponents.

The Haverim were punctilious about ceremonial ablutions like washing the hands and kitchen utensils.[10] We have seen how Jesus dealt with some of these issues in earlier chapters. They tithed on all that they ate, bought or sold and even, as Jesus observed, on common garden herbs.[11] They did not eat with ordinary folks lest something had not been tithed and some items they would not buy from or sell to them.

Were the Pharisees who raised these matters with Jesus, members of the exclusive society of Haverim? Who could function spiritually within such restrictions? Is this what Jesus had in mind when he talked about the burdens they imposed and the way they closed the kingdom of God to themselves and, worse still, to others?[12]

Regarding Sabbath observance, the command against work on the Sabbath was given in the context of the building of the Tabernacle.[13] In consequence, the Oral Law defined work according to every process involved in making the Tabernacle. It listed thirty-nine types of work associated with agriculture, skins, cloth, metal, wood and so on. Each category was then sub-divided into thirty-nine more activities, making one thousand, five hundred and twenty-one in all.

Many regulations strike us as ludicrous. Dragging an object across an earth floor was akin to ploughing. Plucking a few ears of corn and rubbing the husks away was like reaping and winnowing.[14] No wonder Jesus' healing on the Sabbath elicited such a petty response from the Pharisees.[15]

Few people could cope with the scrupulous adherence to the law imposed by the Pharisees. They in turn saw the ordinary people as sinners and kept aloof from them although they always worshipped in the synagogues together. They called them the *am ha'aretz*, literally 'people of the land' or peasants but more pejoratively, boors. Even Hillel, who was noted for his tolerance, once stated that no *am ha'aretz* could be truly pious.

Perhaps the Pharisees had this thought in mind when they disparaged the people who were coming to Jesus, saying, 'This crowd who do not know the law, are accursed'.[16] It says much for the restraint of the despised, impious *am ha'aretz* that on one notable Sabbath day they waited until its end at sundown before the whole city came to Jesus seeking cure for its sick.[17]

Whatever some of the Pharisees were like in New Testament times, they began as a movement of true religious conviction. Even in the gospels, not all Pharisees were fanatics. Some became followers of Jesus, like Nicodemus.[18]

Some made what we must assume were initially sincere overtures as they sent delegations to hear his teaching[19] and invited him to eat in their homes.[20] Yet others respected him sufficiently to warn him of danger to his life.[21] At times they even disagreed amongst themselves about him. Some said that he was a sinner whilst others asked how a sinner could do the wonderful things that he did.[22]

Scribes

Scribes and Pharisees are so often mentioned together that the terms seem interchangeable. Not so! The Pharisees were a religious party. The scribe represented a profession which existed in every society. He copied sacred writings and recorded historical events as we noted in a previous chapter.[23]

Not all scribes worked in a palace library or temple. Some sold their services in the markets and read or wrote letters and legal documents for the illiterate. The itinerant scribe carried a board on which to rest the parchment as he wrote with a quill pen. The ink was made from lamp soot and was kept in a portable inkwell, sometimes attached to the board. It had a lid to prevent spillage.

The psalmist compared his tongue to the pen of a ready scribe.[24] A ready scribe was skilled in his job and wrote quickly and accurately. The psalmist obviously felt that his words flowed fluently as he composed and sang his songs.

As far back as Ezra, the scribes who copied the Scriptures also studied the Torah and taught others.[25] In Jesus' day they were experts in Oral Torah without necessarily being copyists of Scripture. The New Testament variously calls them judges, lawyers and doctors of the Law. Like the Pharisees, they were synagogue elders and members of the local religious leadership.

Some scribes were famous scholars. They had their own schools of followers who learned from them and often argued with each other over points of interpretation. Two such were Hillel and Shammai who lived under Herod the Great. It was not strange that Jesus had his own disciples, some of whom had left their professions to be with him. Nor was it entirely unusual that they were supported by rich women.[26] It was all part of the religious system of the day.

In terms of their beliefs and way of life, the scribes and Pharisees had everything in common. At the same time, although many scribes did become Pharisees, not every scribe was a Pharisee nor was every Pharisee a scribe. This is why some passages specify that the scribes in question were Pharisees.[27] Both groups revered the Oral Torah. Members of both parties made common cause against Jesus. His criticisms of the one apply equally to the other.

In 70 CE Rome quelled a Jewish rebellion and destroyed Jerusalem and the Temple. Almost every group disappeared, not only minor sects but even the influential Sadducees. Not so the scribes and Pharisees! Their leaders regrouped and took decisions which adapted Judaism to the new state of affairs. As we have seen elsewhere, they ensured its survival, centred round the synagogue, and continued to propagate the principles of Oral Torah. Mainstream Judaism has developed up to the present day in a direct chain of tradition from the scribes and Pharisees whom Jesus knew.

Who Crucified Jesus?

Only too often, Christians have blamed Jewish people for the death of Jesus. If pressed to be more specific, they would pick out the priests and the scribes and Pharisees. Ultimately, the gospels implicate every group in the crucifixion; the Sanhedrin, the chief priests who were Sadducees, the elders who were either scribes or Pharisees and also king Herod who came from a proselyte background.[28]

Nor do we forget the role of the Gentile authorities under Pontius Pilate.[29] Indeed, should not the greatest blame lie with Pilate? The Jewish authorities genuinely felt that Jesus was a threat to their ideologies and aspirations. Pilate publicly asserted his belief that Jesus was innocent, then deliberately condemned him to death just the same. He alone had the power to free Jesus. He chose not to.

This is true, yet it all would have come to nothing but for Jesus himself. He offered his life as a willing sacrifice.[30] In the Garden of Gethsemane he relinquished his own will and submitted to God's.[31] At the moment of his arrest, he could have called twelve legions of angels to his defence.[32] Not even Pilate could have had any power over him had God not given it into his hands for that moment.[33]

Peter offers the final summation in one of his first public sermons.[34] He not only indicts Pilate and the Jewish leadership, he also claims that Jesus suffered in the fore-ordained will of God[35] to fulfil God's salvation purposes for the world. You and I are responsible too.

Bible references

1	Mark 7:8	12	Matthew 23:4,13,14	26	Luke 8:2,3
2	Luke 11:37–42	13	Exodus 31:1–12	27	Mark 2:16, Luke 5:30
3	Acts 23:6,7		35:1–19		Acts 23:9
4	Mark 12:18–27	14	Mark 3:4,5	28	Matthew 26:57–59
5	Matthew 16:1	15	Mark 3:4,5		Mark 14:53–55
6	John 11:47,48	16	John 7:49		Luke 22:66, 23:7–11
7	Matthew 27:18	17	Mark 1:29–34	29	Matthew 27:11–26
	Mark 15:10	18	John 3:1, 7:50, 19:39	30	Hebrews 10:5–7, 10
8	John 11:47, 18:3	19	Luke 5:17		Mark 10:45
9	Acts 22:3	20	Luke 7:36, 11:37, 14:1	31	Matthew 26:42
	Philippians 3:6	21	Luke 13:31	32	Matthew 26:53
10	Matthew 15:2	22	John 9:16	33	John 19:10, 11
	Mark 7:4–8	23	Ezra 6:1–5, Esther 6:1	34	Acts 4:27–31
11	Luke 11:42	24	Psalm 45:1 RSV	35	Psalm 40:7
		25	Ezra 7:11, 8:1–9		

Groups Jesus Knew

There were many sects and parties in the first century Jewish community for Judaism was sufficiently vibrant to encompass deviation. Indeed, it drew inspiration from the interaction of divergent ideas. We have already considered three of the most influential groups, the scribes, Pharisees and Saducees, in the last chapter. The New Testament refers to a number of others and we examine some of them below.

Priests and Levites

A simple summary of scriptural teaching traces the origin of the priests and Levites to the time of the Exodus. In the last plague, Israel's firstborn were saved by applying a lamb's blood to their doorposts. Thereafter, God claimed all Israel's firstborn males as his own.[1] The implication was that these were the men chosen to carry out the religious rituals of the nation.

God later transferred the privilege to the whole tribe of Levi because it alone had stood by Moses in the matter of the golden calf.[2] The business was settled in an exact exchange of Levite males for all the firstborn sons of the other tribes. The 273 firstborn in excess of the Levites were bought back from God, or redeemed, for five shekels each.[3]

The distinction between priests and Levites lay in their line of descent from Levi, one of Jacob's twelve sons. Levi had three sons; Gershon, Kohath and Merari. Moses and Aaron came from Kohath's branch by Amram.[4] Aaron and his sons were Israel's first priests and the priesthood was vested solely in Aaron's family ever after.

In the widest sense of the term, anyone who was descended from Levi was a Levite. This included the priests. In the more technical sense of the term, it described all the men who served in the Tabernacle or Temple but who were not priests.

In this connection, we can better understand the motive behind the rebellion of Korah, Dathan and Abiram.[5] The Exodus genealogy shows that Korah was also descended from Kohath but by Izhar.[6] Surely his family had as much right to be priests as Aaron's. Dathan and Abiram were descendants of Reuben and he was Jacob's firstborn.[7] Should they not take precedence over anyone from the tribe of Levi? The story shows how God dealt

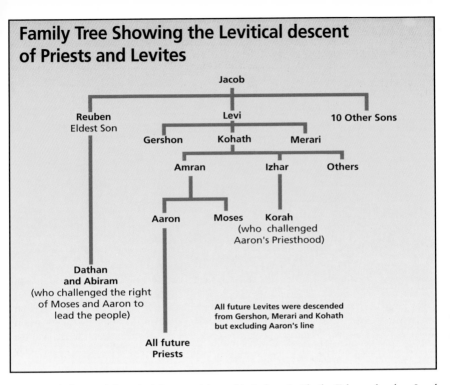

Family Tree Showing the Levitical descent of Priests and Levites

- Jacob
  - **Reuben** — Eldest Son
    - **Dathan and Abiram** (who challenged the right of Moses and Aaron to lead the people)
  - **Levi**
    - **Gershon**
    - **Kohath**
      - **Amran**
        - **Aaron** → All future Priests
        - **Moses**
      - **Izhar**
        - **Korah** (who challenged Aaron's Priesthood)
      - **Others**
    - **Merari**
  - **10 Other Sons**

All future Levites were descended from Gershon, Merari and Kohath but excluding Aaron's line

with the rebellion and the principle was established of a levitical (from Levi) priesthood, but limited to Aaron's line.

The priests looked after all the main services of the Tabernacle and, later, of the Temple. We have already listed their main duties in the chapter on the Temple. In earlier days, they taught the Law and, in hard cases, helped to determine it.[8] They also consulted the Urim and Thummin, which was a system of casting lots to discover God's will for the nation.

Numbers Chapter 4 lists the duties of Levites who were not priests. The other descendants of Kohath, who were not of Aaron's line, carried the altar and the ritual objects from inside the Tabernacle when Israel broke camp. The Gershonites carried the curtains and coverings of the Tabernacle and its courtyard. The Merarites looked after the framework of posts, bars and sockets. When not on the move, they did all that was needed to ensure the smooth running of the sanctuary.

In many ways, the roles of priest and Levite degenerated, particularly if some of the tales in Judges and elsewhere are typical.[9] In later centuries, the northern kingdom of Israel distanced itself from the Temple and set up its own shrines where anyone could pay to become a priest.[10]

In other ways, the roles of the priests and

Levites also developed, as we see from David's plans for the organisation of the new Temple.[11] He divided the families of the priests into a rota of twenty-four sections to serve at the shrine in turn, week about. From the Levites, he arranged similar rotas of cantors, choirs, instrumentalists and gatekeepers. Others were responsible for security and for the Temple treasuries and financial business. Even at the time of Jesus, in the Second Temple, the basic system remained the same.

During the persecutions of the 2nd century BCE, some high priests were deposed in favour of men who were not direct heirs to the position. Caiaphas, who tried Jesus, was a descendant of the Hasmoneans. They took on the title of king, although they were not of the tribe of Judah. They also claimed the office of high priest, to which they had no right because their ancestor, Mattathias, was only a country priest.

Without the Temple, the work of the priests and Levites ceased; yet to this day, relics of their function persist. People surnamed Cohen, Levi, or variations of both, claim priestly descent. They take precedence in the order of the public reading of the Torah in the synagogue. On special occasions they pronounce the priestly blessing[12] over the congregation. They also act in the rite of *pidyon haben*, the redemption of the firstborn son.

The Herodians

When Herod the Great died, Rome divided his kingdom amongst three of his sons. Archelaus became ethnarch of Judaea, Idumea (Edom) and Samaria. Herod Antipas was tetrarch of the Galilee region and Philip was tetrarch of Trachonitis, an area to the north and east of Galilee.

Such was the tyranny of Archelaus that Joseph avoided Judaea when he left Egypt.[13] He returned to Nazareth in Galilee where Herod Antipas ruled. Herod Antipas is the same Herod who married his brother Philip's wife and who beheaded John the Baptist.[14] Apparently, this Philip was not Philip the tetrarch of Trachonitis, as we might suppose.[15] He was another half brother. The family tree of Herod the Great's descendants is complicated and sons of his different wives sometimes shared the same name, as in this case.

Rome soon deposed Archelaus and replaced him with its own governors or procurators, of whom Pontius Pilate was one. Herod Antipas and Philip ruled throughout Jesus' lifetime. Jesus called Herod Antipas a fox, when some Pharisees warned him that Herod wanted to kill him.[16] He appeared before, and was mocked by, this same Herod in his trial. The incident united Pilate and Herod who had previously been at enmity with each other.[17]

King Agrippa I was Herod the Great's grandson. He grew up in Rome and in 37 CE the Emperor gave him the tetrarchy of Trachonitis and the title of king. His domains later extended to Galilee and Judaea. When in Rome he had lived as a Roman but on returning to the country of his origins, he behaved as a strict Jew. He it was who killed James by the sword[18] and who imprisoned Peter and executed the guards on account of his miraculous escape.[19]

Agrippa I collapsed during a public display of grandeur and died in great pain.[20] From the Acts version of the story, we might assume that he died immediately. It is Josephus who records that he died five days later. Also according to Josephus, he wore a silver robe on this occasion which so dazzled the crowd in the rays of the sun that they hailed him as a god. This happened in 44 CE.

His son, Herod Agrippa II, was only seventeen when his father died. At first he was deemed too young to have jurisdiction over the whole area and ruled over Trachonitis alone. He received other territories later.

His sister, Drusilla, was the wife of Felix, the Roman procurator who tried Paul in Caesarea.[21] He had an incestuous affair with another sister, Bernice. When Festus succeeded Felix as procurator, he invited Agrippa II and Bernice to help him judge the case against Paul.[22] Josephus corresponded with him and he died around 100 CE, the last ruler of the Herod dynasty.

It seems, therefore, that the Herodians were a political party which supported the ruling descendants of Herod the Great. Perhaps they even desired to reunite Herod's old kingdom under a ruler of his dynasty who was either strong enough to overthrow Rome or at least to rule with minimal interference from Rome.

All this is interesting in view of the fact that the Herodian dynasty was not strictly Jewish. Herod the Great and his father, Antipater, were Idumaeans (Edomites) who had converted to Judaism. All along and from the very beginning, each ruler held his position by courtesy of Rome.

The Herodians were realistic enough to make the best of the situation as it was. Outwardly they made some show of conforming to Jewish ritual observance and some were no doubt sincere. At the same time, the rulers and their supporters generally co-operated with the Roman authorities. In this respect they were akin to the Sadducees but they followed the scribes and Pharisees in their interpretation of the Law. The party must have been fairly small, comprising members of the Herod family and a few of their friends.

The Herodians joined in the opposition to Jesus, not so much from religious sympathy but because they felt he was a potential threat to their interests. They misunderstood the significance of his kingdom teaching and his messianic claims. They only saw how popular he was with the masses, something Herod's dynasty never had been, and feared where it might lead.

The Herodians are mentioned three times in the gospels. On two of these occasions, which were perhaps the same incident, the question about paying taxes to Caesar comes up.[23] Neither party could catch Jesus out but the Pharisees' willingness to co-operate against him with people whom they normally despised, shows how deeply they hated him.[24]

The Zealots

The Zealots were a sect founded by Judas of Gamala. Gamala was a town which lay a few miles east of the Sea of Galilee, on the high ground overlooking the gorge of the Yarmuk river. Judas headed the opposition to a census imposed by Quirinius, governor of Syria, in 6 or 7 CE. Quirinius is, of course, mentioned in connection with the earlier census at the time of Jesus' birth.

Another name for the Zealots was the Cananaeans, from the Hebrew word for zealous. One of the apostles was Simon the Zealot.[25] In older translations of the Bible he is also called a Canaanite, which seems to be a version of the same term.[26]

The Zealots vehemently resented the Roman domination while fervently awaiting the messianic hope. Unlike the Pharisees, who believed that the messianic kingdom would only come through God's intervention, the Zealots wanted to fight for it. Zealot idealism ranged from mild activism to excessive fanaticism. Some of them raised small, local disturbances against the authorities. Others committed murder. Not a few were caught and crucified for their activities.

Their violence climaxed in the Jewish revolt against Rome and this led to the siege and fall of Jerusalem in 70 CE. Many of their fellow countrymen deplored their extremism which hastened the disaster and increased the severity of the subsequent punishments. Throughout history and to the present time, there are Jewish people who still blame them for their role in that disaster.

Two disciples carried swords in the Garden of Gethsemane. Peter had one and he used it.[27] Did Peter have Zealot sympathies? Who had the other sword? Was it Simon the Zealot? If so, why did he not use it in accordance with his creed? The question does bring home to us the inner turmoil of a man like Simon. It could not have been easy for him to come to terms with Jesus' teaching about the kingdom of God and his programme for its attainment.

Jesus spent forty days after the resurrection teaching his disciples about many things in the light of his passion.[28] In spite of their growing understanding of his ways, and even though most of them were not Zealots, at the very moment of his ascension they were still asking when he would restore the kingdom to Israel.[29]

The Samaritans

In 722 BCE Samaria, the capital of the the northern kingdom of Israel, was conquered by the Assyrians. The Assyrians transported the local people elsewhere and replaced them with foreign colonists from Cuthah, Ava, Hamath and Sepharvaim.[30] These groups became the Samaritans. Josephus says they were called Cutheans in Hebrew and Samaritans in Greek.

The explanation of their origins in 2 Kings tells how they brought their own gods with them. Because things did not go well at first, a Jewish priest was sent to teach them how to worship the God of their new land. This resulted in their adopting a mixture of religious practices; a process known as syncretism.

In 586 BCE, Jerusalem and the southern kingdom of Judah fell to the Babylonians. They imposed the same deportation policy but, in this case, some of the exiles eventually returned after the Persian Cyrus issued his decree in 536 BCE. Later, Nehemiah became governor in Jerusalem. His priorities were to establish the Jews securely back in their own country and to rid Judaism of all foreign and heathen influences.

By this time the Samaritans had been over 200 years in the land and were firmly settled. They would have made alliance with the returning Jews but Nehemiah opposed it on the grounds that they were not Jews and did not worship the Jewish God in the right way. They denied both charges and thereafter did all they could to hinder Nehemiah.[31]

Mutual enmity persisted. Josephus tells how the Samaritans captured Jews as slaves and seized their lands. They put dead bodies into the Temple courtyards and killed Galileans who passed through Samaria on their way to

Israelite remains at the ancient site of Samaria.

Jerusalem. On the other side, John Hyrcanus destroyed the city of Samaria and their temple on Mount Gerizim in 120 BCE. Herod the Great tried to gain their favour by rebuilding their temple and refortifying Samaria. His son, Archelaus, under whose jurisdiction they came, treated them exceptionally cruelly.

Another story concerns the Jewish custom of lighting a chain of bonfires to signal the sighting of the new moon in Palestine to the Jewish diaspora in Babylon. This meant that both communities observed the beginning of the month and its subsequent festivals at the same time. Once, the Samaritans lit false bonfires and set everything in disarray. With its strict emphasis on right observance, this was more serious for Judaism than we might appreciate. Rather than risk the same debacle again, the authorities developed another way of doing things.

With such a history of terrible violence, no wonder the Samaritans and Jews feared and

hated each other and travellers between Galilee and Judaea preferred the Jordan valley route to the quicker way through Samaria. Even Jesus only went through Samaria occasionally.[32] Otherwise he went along the Jordan valley and up to Jerusalem through Jericho.[33] It also emphasises the insult to Jesus in the accusation, 'You are a Samaritan and you have a devil'.[34]

Significantly, Jesus commanded his disciples to take the gospel to Samaria after Jerusalem and Judaea and before going to the rest of the world.[35] As he had tried to show in his story about the Good Samaritan, the two peoples were neighbours and they had a duty to care for each other.

Incredibly, the Samaritan community has survived to the present day. Although they have suffered from centuries of intermarriage, a few hundred people still live on the outskirts of Nablus (biblical Shechem) on the slopes of Mount Gerizim. They no longer have a temple but each Passover they sacrifice lambs on the summit of the mountain. Their ancient Torah scroll is also of great interest to scholars.

In addition, just a few Samaritans live in Holon, a coastal town south of Tel Aviv in Israel. After 1948, the two groups were cut off from each other. Since the Six Day War in 1967, they now have access to each other. Marriage between the two groups, and also with a few Jewish women, has helped to revitalise the community.

The Essenes

The Essenes are not mentioned in the Bible but as some people think that John the Baptist might have been one, we discuss them briefly. According to Josephus they arose from the Hasidim at the same time as the Pharisees.

Philo described them as a saintly sect, numbering about four thousand. He tells how at first they lived in villages and followed agriculture and peaceful trades. They did not have slaves or amass wealth but preferred to share their goods and to support the sick and aged. They studied and kept the Torah but, above all, they emphasised the importance of ritual purity.

Since the discovery of the Dead Sea scrolls in 1947, the Essenes have been identified with the Qumran community. Most tourists visit Qumran, an archaeological site at the edge of the Judaean desert, overlooking the Dead Sea. There they see the scriptorium where members of this community are believed to have copied parts of the Scriptures and to have authored many other works.

The best-known example, in an excellent state of preservation, is the scroll of Isaiah. Tourists can see it in a museum in Jerusalem called the Shrine of the Book. The community hid the scrolls for safety when the Romans destroyed Jerusalem. Nearby are the almost inaccessible caves where the scrolls were discovered.

Many scrolls still await decipherment. Much controversy surrounds this process, as well as the interpretation of those which have been translated and their significance for both Christianity and Judaism. These matters are well documented and can be pursued elsewhere, but with care. The experts hold that some recent, popular works about the scrolls are neither scholarly nor accurate.

It seems that there were two groups of Essenes. Some lived restrictive but normal lives in their own villages. Others retreated into celibacy and monasticism. Pliny the Elder and Josephus, both contemporaneous with the closing days of Qumran, speak about the Essene community on the west of the Dead Sea which could only be joined after three years' probation.

The Essenes who resided there lived simple, celibate lives with many purification rituals and a minute observance of the Torah which not even the strictest Pharisee could cavil at. Their beliefs are best determined through the Dead Sea scrolls themselves. They tended to a dualism of opposites; truth and falsehood or Sons of light and Sons of darkness.

They saw their withdrawal into the wilderness, away from ungodly society, as part of the process of bringing in the Day of Redemption for the world. Their authority for this was Isaiah's statement, 'A voice cries, "Prepare in the wilderness a way for Yahweh [the Lord]—"'.[36]

Part of the community buildings, Qumran. The Essene sect probably formed this settlement.

John the Baptist, as forerunner of the Messiah, claimed to be doing just that and quoted Isaiah to prove it. The emphasis is subtly different in the gospel translation of this passage. John says that he is as Isaiah prophesied, 'A voice that cries in the wilderness, "Make a straight way for the Lord."'[37] Either way, the Essene understanding that preparation for the Messiah had to start in the wilderness was preserved.

John preached a baptism of repentance which was a basic Essene idea. They constantly urged the people to repent before the coming, apocalyptic Day of Judgement. Their baptism was normal immersion in a *mikveh* but, to be effective, a baptism of repentance had to be accompanied by the cleansing of the soul through right conduct. One Dead Sea scroll then states that the repentant sinner will be cleansed from his sins by the spirit of holiness.

Connection between ritual immersion, or baptism, and the work of the Spirit is familiar to New Testament readers. God's Spirit came upon Jesus in a unique way at his baptism.[38] When the Spirit fell upon Cornelius and his friends, Peter's first reaction was that they must be baptised.[39]

In Ephesus, Paul met some disciples of John who knew his baptism of repentance but nothing more. They claimed that they had never heard of such a thing as the Spirit. Another translation might more accurately say that they did not know that the Spirit had yet been given.[40] Popular Jewish tradition believed that an outpouring of the Spirit would accompany the messianic age. These men were actually saying that they did not know that the Messiah had already come

John the Baptist could hardly have spent his early life in the Judaean wilderness without some contact with the Essenes and some knowledge of their teachings. Even if he was never a member of their community, he surely must have known those who lived in ordinary villages and have sympathised with their ideals. John had an ascetic bent and preached repentance and baptism but even there he differed. He sent the penitents, not into asceticism, but back to their homes and jobs to behave in a better way.[41]

As the Essenes were sincere and kept out of the public domain, Jesus had no reason to single them out for condemnation. He must have known about them but could not have been one himself. He was too socially involved with people. The Essenes held aloof from Temple life, Jesus did not. They would also have deplored his practice of ritual purity. Even if his teaching had points in common with theirs, it sprang from a different source and pointed in a different direction.

Bible references

1	Exodus 13:1, 2,11–16	15	Luke 3:1	30	2 Kings 17:24–31
2	Exodus 32:25–29	16	Luke 13:31, 32	31	Nehemiah 4:1–5
3	Numbers 3:11, 39–51, 8:16–22	17	Luke 23:6–12	32	John 4:4
4	Exodus 6:16, 18, 20	18	Acts 12:1, 2	33	Mark 10:32, 46
5	Numbers 16	19	Acts 12:18, 19	34	John 8:48
6	Exodus 6:18, 21	20	Acts 12	35	Acts 1:8
7	Numbers 16:1	21	Acts 24:24	36	Isaiah 40:3
8	Deuteronomy 17:8, 9	22	Acts 25:13–27	37	John 1:23
9	Judges 17—18	23	Matthew 22:16; Mark 12:13	38	Mark 1:9–11
10	1 Kings 12:31; 13:33; 2 Chronicles 13:9	24	Mark 3:6	39	Acts 10:44–48
11	1 Chronicles 23—26	25	Luke 6:15; Acts 1:13	40	Acts 19:1–7
12	Numbers 6:22–27	26	Matthew 10:4 KJV	41	Luke 3:10–14
13	Matthew 2:22	27	Luke 22:38; John 18:10		
14	Matthew 14:1–12	28	Luke 24:25–27, 44–48 Acts 1:3		
		29	Acts 1:6–9		

CHAPTER SEVENTEEN

The Last Word

In the Foreword to this book, my stated aim was to inform readers about the Jewish and Middle Eastern background to the Scriptures and, in particular, to portray Jesus in his own times and culture. I hope that I have achieved this aim adequately.

I am very conscious of how much there is to say and how much I have left unsaid. Perhaps such an objective could never be fully realised in a single book. I am also aware of how selective I have been in the material chosen to illustrate various points. Naturally, the choice of such material was based on the things I know about and have studied but there was one other resource.

I have enjoyed the inestimable privilege of living and working in Israel for twelve years. I have personally seen, and lived through, many things which have brought the Bible to life in unexpected and wonderful ways. It is these individual experiences which I have drawn upon to share with my readers.

Before drawing to a conclusion, there is a very important question to ask. If Jesus was so totally Jewish in the terms of his own age and society, why have the Jewish people so consistently rejected him throughout the centuries?

Faith or Reason

The first reason is theological. Jewish people cannot accept that Jesus is divine. The idea is blasphemous to them. Other aspects of his life and teaching, such as the resurrection, are equally hard to take.

Throughout the centuries, Jewish people have looked for a Messiah who will be a wonderful figure, empowered by the spirit of God in a unique way. He will even have a special relationship with God as his father. In no way, however, will this make him divine or confer upon him any measure of equality with God. He is human, and nothing more.

Most Christians are conditioned from childhood, or from their earliest days as believers, to believe the story of the virgin birth and the incarnation and all that they imply in terms of Jesus' unique relationship with God. We cannot wipe out our conditioning but, if we try to set it aside and put ourselves in the place of our Jewish friends, we must surely see how incredible these things are in the light of plain reason.

We must never forget that we only believe and endeavour to comprehend such incalculable mysteries through the faculty of faith. We cannot even explain what faith is. Why do some people attain to it? Why does it appear to others as foolishness or as some illogicality in the processes of the mind? If we leave faith out of the reckoning, then is not the Jewish understanding of these things the more rationally acceptable?

Messianic Expectations

A second reason why Jewish people reject Jesus is more practical, despite having theological overtones. Jesus is not the awaited, Jewish Messiah because he does not fulfil traditional, messianic expectations.

In his own day, people looked for a political deliverer from the Romans who would restore sovereignty to Israel. He would inaugurate a universal reign of peace, justice and righteousness which even the Gentile nations would acknowledge. People like the Zealots and Pharisees, and even the disciples, had their own ideas as to how this would be accomplished and what roles they would play in the coming kingdom. Sadly, Jesus did not fulfil their hopes and, therefore, for most of them, he was not the Messiah.

The picture is little changed today. There is no universal rule of peace, righteousness and justice in the world. Rather, the opposite is the case. Faced with such clear evidence to the contrary, how can Jesus remotely be the Messiah of Jewish yearnings?

Christians have an answer. They say that Jesus brings peace to the lives of individuals. How true this is! They speak about the Second Coming of Jesus when he will finally judge the world and restore to all things, including mankind, the perfection of the orig-

inal creation. Once again, if we try to be unbiased and set aside our conditioning, does it not sound like a far-fetched excuse to anyone who is looking for these things literally and here and now?

The things which we Christians experience and believe by faith are very real and precious to us but they are not easy for other people to comprehend. This is especially so when the behaviour of Christians fails to match up to the standards they preach. On that note, we come to the main reason why Jewish people have difficulty in trusting in Jesus.

Actions speak Louder than Words

Jewish people want nothing to do with Jesus because of the way Christians have treated them down the ages.

Whole volumes have been written about antisemitism. It has been rife from earliest times and in many forms. Tragically, it has occurred most virulently at the hands of so-called Christians. Although Jews in Moslem lands have been persecuted and discriminated against on many occasions, it is usually acknowledged that Christian regimes have treated them more harshly than any other.

We cannot go into details about the sufferings of the Jewish people, mostly instigated by the church, at the hands of Christians and in the name of Christ. Suffice to say that they have been made the scapegoats for troubles ranging from the black death to economic disasters. They have had their assets confiscated and been expelled penniless from their homes and countries. They have been subjected to torture, rape and murder.

When the Crusaders marched across

Remains of the Crusader fort at Caesarea, built to defend the Christian conquests in Palestine.

Europe to deliver the Holy Land from Moslem domination, they also decided to eliminate the Jewish 'Christ killers' whom they encountered en route. This was one of the most terrible periods in Jewish history.

During the Inquisition, many Jews were 'persuaded' to convert to Christianity. The alternative was often torture and death. If they were consequently suspected of returning to their own religion, they were condemned and burned to death in a public spectacle known as an *auto-da-fe*.

On Good Friday, the priests regularly preached rabble rousing sermons against the 'Christ killers', with the result that the congregations rushed out from the churches to start pogroms in the Jewish quarters of surrounding towns and villages. Jewish families dreaded Easter above all other times of year.

In some places, Jewish babies were forcibly baptised and then taken from their parents and reared in monasteries and convents. Whole communities were herded into churches and forced to listen to sermons aimed at converting them to Christianity. In our own generation, Hitler would have wiped out the whole race completely if he could have done so.

These are but a few examples of the afflictions imposed upon Jewish people in the name of Jesus and the church. We may say that no truly born again Christian would behave in such a way. Whether this is true or not, can we imagine how it sounds to Jewish ears? Yet again, does it not seem like another excuse, a piece of special pleading?

We Christians must acknowledge two

things. Firstly, even if we were not personally involved in the events of the past, the principle of group responsibility forces us to share the church's corporate guilt. In the same way, men like Daniel[1] and Nehemiah[2] took upon themselves the guilt of their nation as they made confession and pleaded for forgiveness and national restoration.

Secondly, we must recognise that, however distasteful the truth, the damage is done. As one lady, whose English was limited, expressed it most vividly, 'You Christians have made Jesus dirty'. There is no excuse. Not even our grief and repentance can obliterate the hurts of the centuries. If most Jewish people prefer to have nothing to do with Jesus, we are to blame.

Volte Face

In 1948 the State of Israel came into being. Almost immediately, Jews everywhere felt themselves take on a new stature. Israel gave them standing and security. This was not only in political terms. It touched the emotions and the very spirit of individual, human beings.

Amongst the many things that happened as a result was the fact that Jewish people began to face issues which they could only avoid in the past. The matter of Jesus was one of them; not Christianity or the church, but Jesus the Jew. At first, the interest in Jesus came from Israelis themselves, then it rapidly spread to other parts of the Jewish world.

Jewish scholars started to study Jesus and his background. The ordinary man in the street felt free to ask questions of his Christian acquaintances. Israeli schools taught about Jesus in the official curriculum. More articles, pamphlets and books on the topic were produced in one ten-year period than in the previous two thousand years. 'Give us back the Jewish Jesus', ran the slogan. 'He was ours before he was yours'.

The academics who studied the life of Jesus used every form of reputable scholarship in their efforts to get behind the gospel narrative and to discover who Jesus was and what he taught and claimed for himself. Their researches are contributing significantly to our appreciation of these things. Moreover, they are invariably sympathetic in their approach and sensitive to Christian susceptibilities. How gracious this is in the light of past history!

We can only select a few things to say about their work. In general they admire Jesus greatly. They consider that he preached an ethical Judaism, more or less in accordance with the Pharisaic teachings. He practised in the tradition of the popular, Jewish, charismatic exorcists and miracle workers of his day who are mentioned in Jewish writings. He aroused the Sadducean establishment and was executed under the Romans for fear of a political uprising.

They conclude that Jesus did not make the claims for himself which his later Christian followers did and which have become part of the basic dogma of Christianity. It was Paul who was mainly responsible for founding Christianity and formulating its doctrinal system. Furthermore, they feel that Paul's Christology is largely rooted in non-Jewish religious perspectives.

They do not shirk the task of examining passages which Christianity uses as proof-texts for its beliefs. In the light of their understanding of their own Jewish traditions, they can usually offer an interpretation which shows that a particular word or text does not necessarily have to be explained in the Christian way. For instance, they say that the title 'Lord' does not need to imply divinity. It was regularly given to persons of standing and authority.

'Son of Man' is another example. As it appears in Daniel, it is an eschatalogical term with overtones of divinity. Christianity follows this interpretation through into the Gospels but there are other ways of viewing it. 'Son of Man' may simply be a substitute for the personal pronoun, 'I', especially in the context of something frightening, awe inspiring or embarrassing. Some scholars feel that Jesus never made the 'Son of Man' sayings at all. They are attributed to him by later followers and writers.

Most of us would probably not agree with all their conclusions but we should not discount them completely, solely because they do not accord with our perceptions of Jesus. The integrity of these scholars is beyond question and so is the value of their research.

Messianic Judaism

Although most Jewish people find that they cannot believe in Jesus, there have always been a few who do. This does not include those who were forcibly converted or who turned to Christianity for reasons of expediency. We are thinking only of those who have sincerely accepted Jesus as their Saviour, Lord and Messiah.

The numbers have always been small and hard to determine because those who truly turned to Jesus were usually expelled from the Jewish community. Perforce, they merged into the Gentile church and tended to lose or hide all Jewish identity. The case, last century, of the European rabbi who came to faith, and most of his synagogue congregation with him, was an unusual exception.

It is only within the last three decades of the twentieth century that Jewish people have begun committing their lives to Jesus in significant numbers. The phenomenon is a diverse work of God's Holy Spirit and cannot be attributed to the activities of any particular church or mission. In most cases, they have become believers in some incidental way, such as through the witness of a friend at work or by casually reading the New Testament.

These Jewish believers in Jesus are found all over the world. Although it is still hard for them, they are not usually cut off completely by their families as was once the case. This means that they can retain their Jewish identity and, even more importantly, develop a new identity as Jewish followers of Jesus. This is expressed in the title which they are generally happy to use of 'Messianic Jews'.

The question of identity is very important and each person has to work it out personally for him or herself. Generally speaking, new Jewish believers want to continue keeping the festivals and observing familiar customs, such as *kashrut* or circumcision. In this way, they maintain relationships with their families. At the same time, they must explore the new dimension which commitment to Jesus opens up in their lives.

Messianic fellowships help them in this respect. There they meet other Jewish people with whom they feel culturally comfortable and share common problems. They may use a little Hebrew in their songs and prayers. They are taught about their new faith whilst being encouraged to see how these things are related to the Jewish faith.

For example, they have no difficulty in appreciating the connection between certain Jewish and Christian festivals, such as Passover and Easter. As a result, they have produced Messianic *Haggadot* (the order of service for the Passover *seder* meal) which incorporate new rituals or adapt some of the old ones in order to explain these links.

Over the years, Messianic congregations and worshipping groups have grown. In the United States of America, some of them have become minor denominations in their own right. In Israel, the numerous small congregations that now exist tend to be autonomous but there is usually good co-operation between them all. Apart from a few exceptions, they are not associated with the Gentile churches in that country.

In most other places, Messianic fellowships take the form of frequent gatherings where like-minded people worship together and support each other. Jewish believers find this helpful because, whatever links they cultivate with Gentile churches, Gentile Christians rarely understand the problems that they have with their families and the Jewish establishment. Nor do they appreciate the desire that they have to preserve their Jewish identity, albeit as Messianic Jews.

In this connection, we must understand how hard it often is for Jewish believers in Jesus to relate to the Gentile church. In one sense, Jewish people live happily in nominally Christian countries and enjoy good relations with their so-called Christian neighbours. At the same time, they are historically conditioned to see Christians as a persecuting enemy. For this reason, however much Messianic believers love and honour Jesus, they do not always find it so easy to draw close to his Gentile followers.

The amazing thing is that, in our own generation, there are Jewish people who are rediscovering the Jewish Jesus who was theirs before ever he was ours.

Final Questions and Considerations

Some people might wonder about the value of such a book as this. Men and women throughout the ages have experienced the saving work of Jesus in their lives without knowing what the traditions of the elders were all about, what the phylacteries and prayer shawl looked like or what happened in the Temple on festive occasions.

Of course faith in Jesus does not depend on knowing what he wore or the prayers he prayed and the social customs he followed. It does depend on who he was and what his life and death accomplished. If this is the case, then do any of the things which we have tried to explain in this work serve any worthwhile purpose? We believe they do, as we hope to show.

Where God is not Mentioned

There is a book in the Bible where the name of God is not once mentioned. It is the book of Esther. Because of this omission it was one of the last books to be officially accepted into the canon of the Jewish Scriptures. Everyone recognised that it told a stirring tale of God's divine providence which ensured the survival of the Jewish people in a time of crisis. Yet, because God's name was not explicitly

Jewish worshippers at Jerusalem's holy Western Wall hold aloft the Torah scrolls.

expressed, a few people felt that the book lacked some measure of spiritual authority.

In terms of practical, daily living, the story of Esther has always been a great source of inspiration and comfort to the Jewish people. Above all, they have turned to it in times of danger and national calamity. Measured on such a scale, its spiritual value is inestimable. In this sense alone, God's name is surely in it and his overruling control is implied in every turn the story takes.

The rabbis offer two helpful explanations for the omission. King Ahasuerus governed a vast area covering many ethnic groups and languages. The story of Esther was told to the Jewish people scattered throughout his empire. It was probably translated into most of their different local tongues. In the process,

God's name could easily be replaced by the name of the deity which was commonly worshipped in a place. This would have been a desecration of his name and character.

Alternatively, the name of the Hebrew God might be transliterated into the local dialect, letter for letter. According to the Jewish understanding of these matters, anyone who then tried to articulate it would have been guilty of profanation.

There was a tradition that none but the high priest knew how to pronounce the four letters making up the sacred name. Moreover, he only did so on special occasions, and in a whisper, so that no one else could hear. To avoid the sacrilege of any heathen uttering God's name, it was better not to use it at all.

The rabbis go further. They say that God's

name does appear in the book of Esther but it is hidden in an acrostic. Acrostics are an accepted biblical usage. The best known is in Psalm 119 where each verse begins with a successive letter of the Hebrew alphabet.

The acrostic in Esther appears in the words, 'Would the king be pleased to come with Haman today to the banquet I have prepared for him?'[3] The Hebrew is very succinct, consisting of four key words. The initial Hebrew letters of these words are *yod, he, vav, he*. Together they make up the sacred name which, to this day, most Jewish people will not pronounce.

As far as this book is concerned, we do not claim any exceptional merit for it. The most we can say is that we have sincerely endeavoured to make Jesus and the Scriptures real and more precious to our readers and, thereby, to bring honour to God's name. On this basis alone, dare we go so far as to hope that if God is present, albeit hidden, in the book of Esther, he will also be present in the pages of this book?

A Man for all Seasons

As we have tried to understand Jesus in the terms of his own age and society, we have seen how different this was from our own days and ways. This vast difference serves to accentuate one, incredible truth about him. Part of Jesus' greatness lies in the fact that he could transcend the provincial bounds of his own cultural norms and offer the world spiritual realities which apply to all ages and peoples.

If we now look briefly at Jesus in this sense, it does not obviate or weaken the importance of what we have wanted to achieve in this work. More often than not, our view of Jesus

focuses on his miraculous acts and divine nature. This book has tried to redress that balance by looking at the human aspects of his life. However, having spent sixteen chapters in this pursuit, it is now good to close by emphasising the following, wonderful truth. Not only was he a man of, and for, his own season, he was 'a man for all seasons'.

Outward circumstances and manners constantly alter. The basic human condition never changes. We eat, sleep, laugh, cry, make love, get ill, grow old and eventually die. We feel pain, pleasure, affection, hatred, fear, desire, anger, jealousy and much more. Jesus speaks to every part of our humanity.

In his life on earth, he not only understood but he actively responded to people's situations. He touched the untouchable leper. He calmed the fear of his disciples by quelling a storm. He comforted a sorrowing mother and raised her only son back to life. He challenged a rich, young man who was already a leader in the community but who felt an emptiness in his life despite his position. He even stepped in to resolve a catering crisis at a village wedding.

Countless men and women, in all periods of history, in all parts of the world and in all positions of life, have put their trust in him and have found that he has spoken to their situation as surely as he spoke to the people of his day. He has resolved problems, given strength to cope in hard circumstances, miraculously removed addictions, changed attitudes and shown the way to take in dark places.

We can say the same about the Bible. If that were not so, why has it been translated into hundreds of languages and why is it still the world's best seller? Every Christian who regularly reads the Bible can testify to times when

An orthodox Jew reads from his Hebrew Bible at Jerusalem's Western Wall.

it has spoken to some personal situation.

How wonderful it is to know that the Jesus who was so totally a product of his own place and time is as relevant to us today as he was to those who knew him then. This is a mystery. We believe it because, like so many people before us, we have proved it for ourselves. That does not mean that we can explain it. Spiritual matters cannot be rationalised or expressed in logical terms but their validity is not in question.

Growth in Grace

Every Christian is on a voyage of discovery. Theologians call it growth in grace. Sadly, for some of us, our Christian understanding stays at a very shallow level. There are times for others of us when we feel that our faith has become humdrum and routine. Perhaps we are spiritually bored. Yet others of us lose an element of sparkle and the enthusiasm that we once had.

No doubt most of us know the things that are necessary to maintain a reasonable standard of Christian living. We do not expect always to stay on the mountain tops. We accept that most of life is lived somewhere on the lower slopes or in the valleys. In other words, we do not look for great thrills and we are content to keep going in a quiet, steady way.

It is our hope that some of the things we talk about in this book will help to revitalise our spiritual lives; and most of us need this at some time or other. Surely it deepens our faith when we learn new things about the Bible and see Jesus in a more accurate perspective. Is it not exciting when a question is answered or a problem solved? Does it not encourage us to explore God's word more deeply and seek after him more urgently?

Old and New Treasures

Jesus often taught the crowds in parables. Some people understood what he meant immediately. For others the parable was merely a good story. Most people gleaned something of its deeper meaning according to their intellectual ability and spiritual insight.

Sometimes the disciples asked Jesus for fuller elucidation which he gladly gave. On one such occasion he asked them if they had understood. He then went on to say, 'Well then, every scribe who becomes a disciple of the kingdom of heaven is like a householder who brings out from his storeroom things both new and old'.[4] Some translations say treasures instead of things and this is a far more emotive word.

Every scribe had a vast knowledge of religious matters, both according to the Written Torah and the Oral Torah. This knowledge was like a priceless treasure. When a scribe became a follower of Jesus, he began to apply his learning to the process of interpreting the new truths which Jesus taught. His understanding of spiritual matters immediately opened up deeper insights into the new teaching. He could then share these with others.

As we have looked at some of the background to the Scriptures and to the life of Jesus, we have seen some of the old treasures of the times and manners of a former age. We hope that, from these old sources, we have succeeded in presenting new insights which will ever challenge the quality of our spiritual standing before God.

Bible references

1 Daniel 9:1–19
2 Nehemiah 1:5–11
3 Esther 5:4
4 Matthew 13:51, 52

INDEX

Page numbers in italics denote illustrations